THE A-LIST DIET & FITNESS PLAN

I dedicate this book to anyone who wants to live a healthier, happier life.
Do stuff, have fun, be nice!

THE A-LIST DIET & FITNESS PLAN

LUKE ZOCCHI

BROLGA
PUBLISHING
www.brolgapublishing.com.au

CONTENTS

INTRODUCTION

This is all about Getting It Done!

Eating well

Training well

Living well

Now!

'Cos if you don't do it now, when will you do it?

I am asked daily: 'How do you stay so motivated to train?' I believe that to stay motivated, you need to see results. When you see the results that come with consistent training and eating habits then you're motivated to continue. That drive to continue keeps producing the results and so it goes on.

Our bodies are amazing machines. We're designed to move, to repair ourselves, to grow and to feel fantastic. In reality, you can't feel good all the time without working at it. But if you feed your body nutritious and delicious food, and put in regular exercise (even if it's hard some days and you don't feel like doing it), you will be buzzing all day and people will start noticing you have that 'buzz' about you.

Life is easy: eat well, exercise regularly and you'll live a long, happy life – right? Ha! That's the theory, but in practice it can feel like it's the hardest thing to do. Everyone knows exercise is important; we all know that a bowl of vegetables is healthier than a bowl of French fries, so why do most of us go for the French fries?

Why are so many people confused about what they should be eating or doing to stay healthy? Why are so many people struggling with being overweight?

How did something that is so simple become so complex?

That's where I come into play. As a personal trainer, and someone who has always been pretty active and health-conscious, I have seen every food and exercise fad under the sun come and go. I've even tried some of them myself.

The turning point for me professionally was when I started training Chris Hemsworth for *Thor*. We used the basic principles required to build muscle and soon we were pretty much two beefcakes walking around pumping iron and getting big.

It was after *Thor 2* that Chris had to drop a lot of weight for his role in *In the Heart of the Sea*. In this movie, the characters get lost at sea and pretty much starve, so we had to work really hard at achieving a look that you wouldn't normally go for! It was hard work, but I learned a lot from the nutritionist on set about nutrition and calorie-restricting diets and what they do to your body.

I had also gotten over the big, muscly look and had started exploring different ways of training to have a fitter and more functional body. I noticed a huge difference when I started shortening my workouts and basing them on high-intensity interval training (HIIT). I felt like I was pushing myself much harder in my sessions, but I was spending less time in the gym than ever and was getting better results. I started playing around with these types of workouts in both cardio and weight-training sessions. I started using them with my clients on set and noticed two things: firstly, that we could actually fit our sessions in between busy filming schedules; and secondly, that they were getting great results.

At the same time, I stripped my nutrition back to basics – no fancy diets or gimmicks, but instead just focusing on eating unprocessed and whole foods. The results were easily some of the best transformations I had seen. For myself, I felt fit and healthy and believed I looked the best I ever had. For the actors, I noticed the same; they were getting great results, making progress and they were telling me how much they enjoyed the sessions. This motivated them to keep going, to look forward to their training sessions.

My experience on film sets, and my own journey in training and nutrition, led me to create my Twenty40 training program online (zocobodypro.com). I developed this program for the everyday person, for busy people who do not have the time to spend hours in the gym. My program focuses on high-intensity interval training (HIIT) and easy-to-follow nutrition principles, making it simple and achievable for anyone to get the results they desire. After all, as my favourite quote (by Tony Robbins) goes: complexity is the enemy of execution. Why make it hard if it doesn't need to be, right?

These days, I am hired to train people – some of whom you might know – because I get great results in a short amount of time. I've used my many years of experience to discover what works best, so I can design programs to be as efficient and easy as possible.

Whether you picked up this book because you want to lose weight, build strength or get fitter, the basics of achievable exercise and nutrition goals are here.

This book is all about achieving your healthiest life. It's not a magic diet or a quick-fix for a perfect body. By combining my simple 20-minute training program (you can do it at home, with no equipment required) with easy and delicious meals that are based on good nutrition (and don't require calorie counting or special supplements) you can become your better self.

Whether you're an A-lister or an Average Joe, you will get the best outcome when you follow a guide that is simple, effective, easy and fun – and with results you can see.

You want to feel alive and pumping with energy! You want to feel so good that you are bursting out of your skin!

So...

LET'S GET IT DONE!

MY WORKOUT PHILOSOPHY

Being motivated to train and actually enjoying a fitness program makes a major difference when it comes to getting results.

I really want to help educate people on the best way to eat and train to get results in a way that doesn't eat into their family time or isolate them from living their everyday life. I created my program based on the workouts I was doing myself and with my clients.

I don't want people to jump on fad diets and spend hours in the gym. I want people to learn how to train smarter and eat in a way to support their training so that they maximise their results. I want people to be able to maintain those results and enjoy living their healthiest life.

Before we jump into things, here is a quick look at my exercise philosophy. All of the workouts are for 20 minutes and can be done from the comfort of your own home, without any special equipment. Combined with the delicious fresh food in the 30-minute recipes, my aim is to improve your overall health, maximise your fat loss and begin toning your body to be strong, healthy and to look and feel great.

FASTED TRAINING

Exercising first thing in the morning before you eat breakfast is a great way to help your body burn fat more efficiently. Our body's main source of energy is carbohydrates and in simple terms our carbohydrate levels are depleted overnight. When we get up in the morning and train first thing, before eating breakfast, we tap into our fat stores much quicker. This is known as fasted training.

HIIT ME UP

HIIT stands for high-intensity interval training. Basically, this means that you do short bursts of high-intensity exercise with alternating rest periods. Training like this is way more effective for fat loss than steady-state cardio and it's done in half the amount of time!

Studies have shown that sustained HIIT training improves cardiovascular fitness and reduces the risk of type 2 diabetes; it may also help prevent four of the top ten disease-related causes of death and, because your overall health and fitness is improved, it can help protect against many other illnesses. It's more time-efficient than normal endurance exercise and produces results more quickly.

Here are some HIIT workouts you can do at the gym:

Treadmill HIIT: 20 seconds work // 40 seconds rest x 20 repetitions
Rowing HIIT: 20 seconds work // 40 seconds rest x 20 repetitions
Bike HIIT: 20 seconds work // 40 seconds rest x 20 repetitions
Battle Rope HIIT: 20 seconds work // 40 seconds rest x 20 repetitions

And here are some HIIT workouts you can do at home:

Running on the spot HIIT: 20 seconds running // 40 seconds rest x 20 repetitions, as well as following the 20-minute HIIT workout plans in this book.

I don't want people to jump on fad diets and spend hours in the gym. I want people to learn how to train and eat smarter.

*Try not to focus too much on the numbers
on the scales. Your body can be changing significantly
and yet your weight can stay the same.*

WARMING UP & COOLING DOWN

It's important to warm up before exercising and cool down afterwards, to prevent injury and combat fatigue.

WARM UP

Make sure you warm up before exercising. This is super important as it helps the blood flow through your muscles and prepares your body to train.

1 // Running on the spot at 50% of your top pace for 1–2 minutes

2 // Go through one round of the workout you're about to do at 50% of your top pace

COOL DOWN

After your workout, make sure you spend 5–10 minutes cooling down, stretching and allowing your heart rate to slow down. Here are some great examples of exercises to do after training.

1 // Spinal twist: Lie on your back with your knees bent and feet flat on the floor. Let your knees fall towards the floor on one side until you feel a stretch in your spine. Hold for 10 seconds and return to the starting position. Repeat on the other side. Repeat 10 times.

2 // Glute stretch: Lie on your back and bend one leg. Straighten your opposite leg and raise it towards the sky. Put the foot of your bent leg on the knee of your straight leg. Pull your straight leg towards your chest. Hold for 30 seconds. Repeat on the other side.

3 // Cobra: Lie face down with your hands under your shoulders. Slowly push your torso up as far as you comfortably can. Hold and then lower to starting position. Repeat 5 times.

4 // Child's pose: Start in a kneeling position. Sit your hips back onto your feet. Stretch your arms and upper body forward and down. Rest your arms in a relaxed position along the floor and rest your forehead on the floor. Hold for 5 deep breaths.

5 // Lunge stretch: Step forward with your right foot into a lunge position. Lower the left knee to the ground. Extend the right knee forward. Press your hips forward until you feel a gentle stretch in your hip flexor. Hold for 5 deep breaths, then repeat on the other side.

6 // Hamstring stretch: Lie on your back. Raise your left leg towards the sky, keeping your pelvis flat on the floor. Hold your thigh and gently pull the leg towards you. Flex your foot and hold for 5 deep breaths, then repeat on the other side.

PROGRESS

Although it's important to measure your progress, try not to focus too much on the scales. Your body can be changing significantly and yet your weight can stay the same. This is because you are gaining lean muscle and losing fat. Taking photos and looking at your overall shape is a better way to see your progress. Take a front-on and side-on photo *before* you start your plan and then regularly as you progress. These images can be kept private or you can share them with me:

@zocobodypro // #twenty40training // #iamabodypro // #getitdone

Change is just a mindset. Just flick that switch in your head and get it done!

Exercising and eating well isn't just about looking good, it's about feeling good too!

BEFORE & AFTER PICS

Here are some success stories from people who have completed my training program. Their weight may not have changed much but their bodies definitely have!

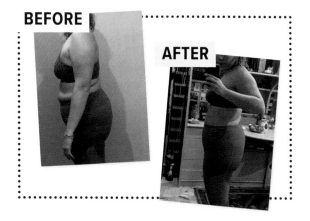

BEFORE

AFTER

BEFORE

AFTER

BEFORE

AFTER

BEFORE

AFTER

BEFORE

AFTER

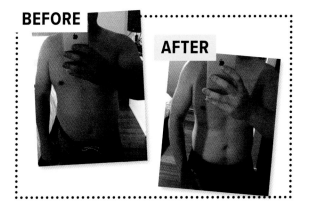

Tag your before and after shots and share with me at #twenty40training #iamabodypro And see more success stories at zocobodypro.com

MY FOOD PHILOSOPHY

My recommended way of eating is NOT a diet. It is NOT a set of restrictions designed to limit your food consumption. It is NOT a set of rules that you must blindly follow. Instead it is about empowering you to make choices: smart, well-informed choices. My 30-minute meals are designed to provide a balanced diet and optimal nutrition without the need for calorie counting.

Understanding the nutritional composition and combination of the foods you eat means you can choose what works best for you to satisfy hunger, promote health and vitality, and provide the vitamins, minerals and amino acids that will enable your body to not only stay alive, but to thrive.

My goal with these guidelines and recipes is to help you create a balanced lifestyle that is accessible and sustainable. If you know how to make healthy choices each day with food and activity you will be strong, healthy and feel amazing.

BACK TO BASICS

My approach to eating is based on eating whole and unprocessed foods. This means foods that are as close to their natural form as possible, avoiding overprocessed foods. Choose fresh, organically grown fruit and vegetables; whole grains such as millet, barley, quinoa and rice or wholemeal (whole wheat) breads and pastas; and herbs and spices that add flavour and antioxidants without adding unnecessary fat or sugar. Protein can be in the form of fish, chicken, lamb, pork or steak. Good sources of vegetarian protein include eggs, cheeses and combinations of vegetable, grain and legume proteins (see Protein for Vegetarians, page 23).

CHANGE

A major part of successfully changing your lifestyle is overcoming old habits. Breaking unhealthy eating habits is not an easy thing to do – it will test you mentally and physically. The key thing to remember is that it will get easier.

It takes 21 days to create a new habit, so after a few weeks you will notice that you stop craving the unhealthy sugars you were eating and are finding your new way of eating normal and easy to follow. You just need to stick with it. Remember why you started this and look at the bigger picture. Of course you will slip up; you will have days where you haven't followed your meal plan. That's OK, it happens; just get back on track with the next meal.

You can train as hard as you want, but if you don't get your diet right, you won't go far.

PREPARATION

Failing to prepare is preparing to fail! We make bad food choices when we are hungry, so it's a good idea to always have meals and snacks prepped and ready so there is good food on hand when you need it.

I personally like to cook my lunch and dinner for the next day the night before and pack them into containers. I lead a very busy life, as I'm sure most of you do, and I find that this is the best way for me to stay on track: having food ready to go when I am hungry and looking for my next meal. I always cook my breakfast and eat it straight away.

This may not necessarily be the best way for you to do your meal prep. I know clients who like to do a big cook-up on a Sunday afternoon and then freeze their meals for their entire week. Either way, being organised will help you stay on a healthy path. Look for recipes labelled 'Make Ahead' in the recipe section to give you a head start.

MEAL PLANNING

OK, here is the most effective formula I've found for meal planning, which has helped me and my clients to get into the best shape of our lives.

I base my meals around my training. This means I choose high-carb meals (clearly labelled 'Post-workout meals' in the recipe section) *only* after I exercise. If I don't train, I don't eat as many carbs and choose the Core (low-carb) meals throughout the day. Why do I do this? Simple: carbohydrates are the body's main form of fuel. When we exercise, we deplete our storage levels of carbs, so the best time to eat them is after we train. However, when we eat an excess of carbs the storage levels overflow and spill into our fat storage. The recipes in this book are all clearly marked as 'Post-workout meals' (high carb) or 'Core meals' (low carb).

I consider good-quality fats (see page 31) to be part of a healthy diet. The only time I reduce my fat intake is for a post-training meal. The reason for this is that fat takes a long time to digest and will slow down the digestion of protein and carbohydrates as well.

I also recommend that you stick to three main meals a day and up to two snacks (optional: only if you feel you need them). This keeps your body's blood-sugar levels stable and prevents you from having a drop in blood sugar, which often leads people to make bad food choices. I recommend eating every three to four hours to avoid this. If you're on a rest day, make sure to choose Core meals. Everyone is different and, if you get hungry between meals, you can choose one of the snacks I've included for a quick and nutritious fix to tide you over until your next meal.

I've also included some indulgent sweet recipes in a chapter I call Sunday Funday, but that doesn't mean it's the only day you're allowed to have them! It's more to say that these are treats and not to be eaten every day. After all, we all need a delicious dessert every now and then.

To maximise the benefits of this program, I recommend you take the time to have a look at the recipes and create meal plans that best suit your lifestyle. Then you can get your preparation happening so that you're ready to eat well all week. The recipes are almost all designed to serve two people, so you can follow my program with your partner or housemate – or be super organised and store the leftover portion for your next meal!

The recipes are based on recommended starting portion sizes. I want you to gauge how your body responds to these meals and how much your body requires to feel satisfied. If the meal feels like it is too big a serve for you, then I encourage you to adapt it to suit your body's needs and make it a little smaller next time. The same goes if you are still feeling hungry after a meal: increase your portion size next time. Everybody is different and it is crucial for you to get to know your body and find out what works best for you. Just be sure you are sticking to whole foods and that you are eating slowly so that you are tasting and enjoying your food. Eating these foods until you are satisfied will mean that you can't go wrong: so get it done!

VEGETARIANS

For those who follow a vegetarian diet, there are still plenty of options in my program (look for the Ⓥ under the recipe title – there are heaps!). Grains and vegetables are not as calorie dense as animal proteins and processed foods but they fill you up more. Eating this way takes up more space in your stomach, which then signals to your brain that you are full.

Although there are not many grains or vegetables that are considered complete protein sources (ones that contain all nine essential amino acids), some combinations will give you tremendous benefits for gaining muscle and staying lean. If gaining more muscle is your goal, then combining this program with a good amino-acid supplement and specific minerals and vitamins will help you reach that goal quicker.

You can add extra protein to any of these recipes with foods such as eggs, protein powders and cheeses in moderation. Try to look for and explore as many vegetables and complete grains as possible. Plant-based foods contain a lot more substance, because they contain more fibre and water than animal-based and processed foods.

Listen to your body and note how you respond to everything. Most importantly, make it taste good!

Carbohydrates for vegetarians

I have been asked if lowering carbohydrates, specifically starches and grains, as a vegetarian trying to get lean on a training program is possible: sure. Is it sustainable? In my opinion, no. Vegetarians require extra nutrients when training, especially if their goal is to gain more lean muscle. Training depletes the body of many nutrients and requires the help of complete foods and supplements to make up for the absence of proteins and amino acids that many vegetables lack.

Specific grains and legumes, along with a variety of vegetables, can help rebuild the body and strengthen the immune system to support the daily stresses and challenges our bodies and minds endure. They also give us sustained energy to power through our workouts and help us maintain focus.

My program is about offering more choices, not taking them away. This is a lifestyle program that will empower you to see the endless possibilities you have to look and feel exactly the way you want. Variety is key and having an unlimited selection of whole and nutritious foods will only make your journey more pleasurable.

Vegetarians require extra nutrients when training, especially if their goal is to gain more lean muscle.

Protein for vegetarians

There are many different opinions out there as to whether protein is absolutely necessary for muscle building and strength development. I believe that it depends on the individual and that it is only by monitoring your goals and how your body reacts to your training that you will be able to truly see what you need. Food choices and supplementation should still be the foundation of your training. I have seen many athletes and people who train hard still gain muscle and strength while following a vegetarian or vegan diet. It is important to consume enough calories along with quality ingredients and proper supplementation.

When it comes to protein powders, there are many vegetable-based ones that are just as good as dairy or animal-based powders. What can make these vegetable protein powders even more powerful is the proper balance of vegetable, grain and legume protein mixed together. Look for pea protein, rice protein and hemp protein powders, which are all available as supplements in most health-food stores.

When choosing your meals, be sure to include a good balance of vegetables, legumes and grains. Make sure your diet includes a wide variety of vegetables, such as broccoli, asparagus, cabbage, zucchini, squash and parsnip. Certain grains, such as quinoa, millet and amaranth, contain all nine essential amino acids, which makes them very similar to most dairy and animal proteins. These ancient grains are also great sources of fibre, which is essential for proper absorption of nutrients.

SAMPLE DAY ON A PLATE

If you're training in the morning, I recommend doing so on an empty stomach (see Fasted Training, page 11). Remember to choose a Post-workout meal (high carb) *after* your training session, whether that is in the morning or afternoon, and Core meals (low carb) at all other times. Stick to three main meals per day plus up to two snacks (but only if you need them). See below for some examples of daily meals.

MORNING TRAINING

BREAKFAST //	Oat pizza with artichoke & havarti (high carb)
MORNING SNACK // (OPTIONAL)	Green banana smoothie
LUNCH //	Classic lamb kebabs with cucumber yoghurt (low carb)
AFTERNOON SNACK // (OPTIONAL)	Honey-bee yoghurt whip
DINNER //	Honey–soy salmon with mushrooms & greens (low carb)

AFTERNOON TRAINING

BREAKFAST //	Cheesy scramble with greens (low carb)
MORNING SNACK // (OPTIONAL)	Spicy jalapeño, chicken & avocado dip
LUNCH //	Bun-less beef burger with melted onions, avo & grilled radicchio (low carb)
AFTERNOON SNACK // (OPTIONAL)	Smashed zucchini on toast with mint, sauerkraut & feta
DINNER //	Seared blue-eye trevalla with herby pasta (high carb)

MORNING TRAINING
VEGETARIAN

BREAKFAST //	Sweet potato pancakes (high carb)
MORNING SNACK // (OPTIONAL)	On-the-go almond protein bar
LUNCH //	Roasted brussels sprout & quinoa salad (low carb)
AFTERNOON SNACK // (OPTIONAL)	Fruit & yoghurt parfait
DINNER //	Spicy walnut tacos (low carb)

AFTERNOON TRAINING
VEGETARIAN

BREAKFAST //	Charred strawberries with yoghurt & muesli (low carb)
MORNING SNACK // (OPTIONAL)	Pineapple power smoothie
LUNCH //	Herbed pumpkin, feta & radish on rye (low carb)
AFTERNOON SNACK // (OPTIONAL)	Smoky eggplant dip
DINNER //	Moreish mushroom & lentil burger (high carb)

YOUR GO-TO FOODS

These are some of the most nutrient-dense and accessible foods that you can consume. They form the basis of all my recipes.

FRESH FRUIT

- Apples
- Apricots
- Avocados
- Bananas
- Blueberries
- Cherries
- Cranberries
- Figs
- Grapefruit

- Grapes
- Kiwifruit
- Lemons
- Limes
- Mangoes
- Melons
- Nectarines
- Olives
- Oranges

- Papaya
- Peaches
- Pears
- Pineapples
- Plums
- Pomegranates
- Raspberries
- Strawberries

Dried fruit

I don't usually recommend eating too much dried fruit because it can be very calorie dense. Most commercially produced dried fruit is made with added processed sugars, which can spike blood-sugar levels, making you more hungry and lethargic. However, there are some available with no added sugars and these can be consumed sparingly if fresh fruit isn't available. Mixing dried fruit with foods high in 'good' fats, such as nuts or avocados, slows down the digestive process of the dried fruit, which helps balance your energy over a longer time and minimises the spikes in your blood-sugar levels.

FRESH VEGETABLES

- Artichokes
- Asparagus
- Beetroot
- Bok choy
- Broccoli
- Brussels sprouts
- Cabbage
- Capsicums
- Carrots
- Cauliflower
- Celery
- Cucumbers
- Eggplants
- Garlic
- Kale
- Leeks
- Lettuce
- Mushrooms
- Onions
- Pumpkin
- Radishes
- Silverbeet
- Spinach
- Squash
- Tomatoes (these really belong to the fruit family, but we usually treat them as vegetables)
- Turnips
- Zucchini

LEGUMES (BEANS & PULSES)

Legumes contain antinutrients; that is, substances that can interfere with the digestion and absorption of nutrients. Soaking dried legumes before eating can eliminate these antinutrients, and rinsing canned varieties removes any preservatives. What is left is an incredibly cheap source of quality nutrition, including a great plant-based source of protein.

- Cannellini beans
- Chickpeas
- Green beans
- Kidney beans
- Lentils
- Peanuts (despite their name, peanuts are not a nut but a legume)
- Pinto beans

Soybeans

I choose to avoid most soybeans and soy products, because many commercial soybean crops are genetically modified and even organically grown soybeans naturally contain antinutrients. Traditional fermentation destroys these antinutrients, which allows your body to enjoy soy's nutritional benefits; however, most of us consume unfermented soy, mostly in the form of soy milk, tofu and textured vegetable protein (TVP). There is a lot of debate about the pros and cons of soy, so I encourage you to do your own research and make your own informed decision about whether to include it in your diet.

DAIRY & ALTERNATIVES

Since the 1970s, the number of people with sensitivity to dairy foods has been growing. If you do enjoy milk, yoghurt and cheese, but can't digest the traditional lactose-based products, look at trying dairy substitutes from sources other than cows. Products from goats, sheep and buffalo also have smaller fat molecules than cattle and so are easier to digest. Organically farmed dairy products may also be easier to tolerate, so seek out small farms that stick to old-fashioned production and pasturing.

- **Almond milk**
- **Cheddar**
- **Coconut milk**
- **Cow's milk (full fat)**
- **Eggs (free-range)**
- **Goat's milk and cheese**
- **Haloumi**
- **Havarti**
- **Hemp milk**
- **Parmesan**
- **Pecorino**
- **Rice milk**
- **Sheep's milk and cheese**
- **Yoghurt** (all types, except for soy based)

Cow's milk

Full-fat milk is much better than skim milk for amounts of CLA, an omega-6 fatty acid that is only found in dairy products and helps with metabolism and fat burning.

FATS

Fats are another source of energy for your body and are vital for regulating hormones and transporting the fat-soluble vitamins A, D, E and K. There is a common misconception that eating fats will make you fat: this is not true! The only time I reduce my fat intake is for a post-training meal. The reason for this is that fat takes a long time to digest and will slow down the digestion of protein and carbohydrates as well.

- **Butter (raw and for cooking)**
- **Ghee (for cooking)**
- **Canola oil (for cooking)**
- **Goat's butter (use raw)**
- **Coconut oil (for cooking)**
- **Grapeseed oil (for cooking)**
- **Extra-virgin olive oil (in dressings)**
- **Olive oil (for cooking)**

NUTS & SEEDS

Nuts provide a range of nutrients, including 'good' fats and protein, fibre and essential vitamins and minerals as well as antioxidants.

- **Almonds**
- **Hemp seeds**
- **Cashew nuts**
- **Macadamia nuts**
- **Chia seeds**
- **Pumpkin seeds**
- **Coconuts**
- **Sesame seeds**
- **Flaxseeds**
- **Sunflower seeds**
- **Hazelnuts**
- **Walnuts**

CARBOHYDRATES

Carbohydrates are the body's main form of fuel. When we exercise, we deplete our storage levels of carbs, so the best time to eat them is after we train. However, when we eat an excess of carbs the storage levels overflow and spill into our fat storage, so the key here is to link your carb intake to how active you are.

BREADS

- Rye
- Sourdough
- Spelt
- Wholegrain

GRAINS

- Barley
- Buckwheat
- Farro
- Millet
- Oats
- Pasta (wholemeal)
- Quinoa
- Rice (see below)
- Spelt

TUBERS

- Jerusalem artichokes
- Sweet potatoes
- Potatoes
- Yams

Gluten

If you suffer from coeliac disease or are gluten intolerant, substitute any bread that suits your dietary requirements. Remember, wheat (gluten) is not the enemy if it is treated properly, especially if it is made with a starter to ferment it, like sourdough. The way the wheat is processed is what can make it difficult to digest. Many commercial breads are highly processed and full of unwanted ingredients.

Brown & white rice

I advocate eating both brown and white rice. Brown rice contains more fibre, but you are better off getting your fibre from more nutrient-dense sources such as fruit and vegetables. While it's true that brown rice contains protein, it's a negligible amount; you're better off with a mouthful of animal protein. There is one thing about brown rice that makes it problematic and that is the presence of phytic acid, a compound located in the rice bran – the part that gives brown rice its colour. Phytic acid, quite simply, grabs onto (or chelates) minerals, in addition to inhibiting enzymes we need to digest food. That's why white rice is often a superior food, especially for athletes. White rice is often fortified with vitamins (digestible ones) and doesn't generally cause the food allergies, bloating or other digestive problems often associated with grains.

PROTEIN

Proteins are essential nutrients for the human body: the building blocks of all our cells. Protein is essential for muscle repair and maintenance. This is why I eat the same portion of protein in my three main meals each day, regardless of whether the meal is a post-training (high-carb) meal or not.

SEAFOOD

Make sure it is wild or sustainably caught.

- **Mackerel**
- **Salmon**
- **Sardines**
- **Shellfish**
- **Trout**
- **Tuna**
- **White firm-fleshed fish (blue-eye trevalla, mahi-mahi, snapper)**

LEAN MEAT

- **Beef (fillet)**
- **Chicken (breast fillet)**
- **Duck (breast fillet)**
- **Lamb (fillet, loin)**
- **Pork (tenderloin)**
- **Turkey (breast fillet)**

HIGHER-FAT MEAT

Moderate consumption of higher-fat cuts of meat is OK, particularly if you are following a low-carb diet.

- **Chicken and turkey (thighs, wings, legs)**
- **Game (buffalo, kangaroo, emu, venison)***
- **Lamb (rack, leg, shoulder)**
- **Pork (chops)****
- **Sausages*****

*These are wild meat options found in many parts of the world. They are increasingly available due to their health benefits and sustainability; so if you see these at your local butcher or market, give them a try.

**Fattier pork cuts, such as bacon, belly and jowl, are best in moderation even if you are following a low-carb diet.

***Sausages made with lean cuts of meat are best, but other higher-fat mixes are fine in moderation and when following a low-carb diet. When selecting sausages, check the ingredients with your butcher. Choose them as a treat rather than a regular meal.

I don't count calories. I simply base my meals around vegetables, lean meats and non-processed carbs.

Don't over-complicate things!

HERBS & SPICES

Fresh or dried spices and herbs are great for adding flavour to your food and most have wonderful nutritional properties as well. For example, turmeric is a natural anti-inflammatory, parsley aids digestion and contains iodine (helping with thyroid function) and cinnamon can help balance blood-sugar levels.

- **Allspice**
- **Basil**
- **Bay leaves**
- **Chilli (fresh, dried flakes and ground)**
- **Chives**
- **Cinnamon**
- **Coriander (leaves and ground seeds)**
- **Cumin**
- **Dill**
- **Ginger (fresh and ground)**

- **Kaffir lime leaves**
- **Mint**
- **Oregano**
- **Paprika (sweet and smoked)**
- **Parsley**
- **Peppercorns (freshly ground)**
- **Sesame seeds**
- **Star anise**
- **Tarragon**
- **Thyme**
- **Turmeric**

Salt

Opinions on salt have changed greatly over recent years. Generally speaking, optimum salt intake varies from person to person depending on lifestyle, diet and overall health. If you are eating balanced wholefood-based meals, then your food will be very low in sodium, so adding salt for flavour is not a problem.

The best salt to consume is natural sea salt that has not gone through any processing to alter its natural make-up. Sea salt contains essential trace minerals that the body needs to be healthy. These trace minerals help build a strong immune system.

Sea salt also helps the digestive system to create juices that break down food faster. This helps prevent sluggish digestion, which can lead to constipation and weight gain.

So ... use salt! SEA SALT. It will benefit you and make your food taste a whole lot better.

SWEETS

In our food, there are five basic tastes that, if included in each meal, will make us less likely to experience cravings or binge eating. These tastes are: salty, sour, bitter, umami (pleasant savoury taste) and sweet.

Balance is the key to living a daily life of good food and fitness, and sweets CAN and should be allowed with moderation. There are choices to be made here about the options that actually work in your favour, bringing nutrition and energy to your body rather than making you feel sluggish or unwell, or leaving you with a craving for empty calories.

Good-quality dark chocolate, for instance, contains antioxidants and minerals. It also helps lower high blood pressure, raise HDL (healthy cholesterol) and protects LDL (the cholesterol that can damage arteries, putting you at risk of heart attack) against oxidation. The caffeine and theobromine found in dark chocolate helps with brain function, and its high amounts of flavanols can help protect your skin from the sun.

There are lots of ways to add sweetness to your food without resorting to highly processed sugars and artificial sweeteners. My recipes use honey, maple syrup (make sure it's 100 per cent pure maple syrup and not the artificial stuff) and rice malt syrup instead of refined granulated sugar. Honey and maple syrup both contain valuable minerals and nutrients, and rice malt syrup is a good slow-release sweetener alternative for those who have difficulty absorbing fructose.

Balance is the key to living a daily life of good food and fitness.

WATER

Water makes up two-thirds of what we are and influences 100 per cent of the processes in our body. By water, I mean PURE water: not tea, coffee, soft drink or juice. Water helps our brain, our skin, it keeps our digestive system moving and reduces the burden on the kidneys and liver by helping to flush out waste products. It is great for cleaning out the colon and preventing constipation. Water helps our joints and cartilage stay hydrated and lubricated. It also keeps our spinal cord and tissues from drying out. Most importantly, water helps our body with the absorption of the nutrients we consume from our foods. It can assist with weight loss and, when consumed before a meal, help control hunger by making us feel fuller, faster. Most people who constantly feel sluggish and fatigued are suffering from dehydration. Think of it this way, if you don't water a plant it shrivels up and dies. So make sure to 'water yourself' every day.

ALCOHOL

If you do not consume alcohol then this will not affect you, but for a lot of people alcohol is an enjoyable part of their social life. Now, I am not recommending that you drink alcohol, but if you choose to do so, then do it smart. Many of us have had those nights when we overconsume and end up not remembering anything except for the extra-large pizza we ate due to hunger induced by an alcohol binge. And what about the morning after? Thumping headaches, giddiness and nausea caused by dehydration. Excess alcohol interferes with fat burning, as well as protein synthesis and muscle metabolism.

This can all be prevented. Firstly, make sure you eat before you drink. Consuming alcohol on an empty stomach not only lowers your blood sugar, it increases your hunger, which is the reason why people lose all discipline with food options. Drinking on an empty stomach also disrupts your digestive system and puts your kidneys and liver into overdrive as they desperately try to burn and dispose of the alcohol.

When you are drinking alcohol, consume a full glass of water (no ice) for every glass of alcohol. Remember, balance is the key: be moderate with your consumption and don't abuse your body.

Beer & wine

Keep in mind that while red wine can aid digestion, it also contains histamine, which can actually increase your appetite and affect your blood sugar. Beer, on the other hand, contains bitter compounds, which, if consumed with food, can help you feel full more quickly. Drinking to excess (whatever you choose to drink) will have a negative impact on your results, so pay attention to how you feel and don't overdo it.

Cocktails

When drinking cocktails, remember that many of them contain sugar, which means extra calories. Be smart about your selection: make sure the mixers are freshly pressed fruit. Try to stick with the natural sweetness of the fruit, but if extra sweetness is necessary, choose natural sweeteners such as honey or maple syrup. Savoury cocktails, which use herbs and spices, are great options as well: the Bloody Mary is an iconic savoury cocktail. Use soda water in place of sugary soft drink mixers. Be sure to eat before drinking, be moderate with quantities, stay hydrated and enjoy.

TEA & COFFEE

If you like your tea and coffee milky, I suggest limiting your intake to one cup per day as the calories in multiple lattes can add up quickly. These little changes can have a big impact on your results.

SUPPLEMENTS

Protein powder: Post-workout shakes are not compulsory for my exercise program, but having a protein shake after training does help with repair and recovery. The benefits are most effective if you have a shake within 30 minutes after training. I go for a clean whey protein or a complete pea protein. Some of the recipes in this book also include protein powder as an optional ingredient.

BCAA: Without getting too technical, Branched Chain Amino Acids are a supplement you can buy that's helpful for maintaining muscle mass. If you are doing fasted training (first thing in the morning before you have any food), I advise taking BCAA to prevent muscle breakdown and also to assist with recovery. It is optional and you can still successfully follow my exercise program without using BCAAs.

Pre-workout: Personally, I don't use a pre-workout supplement. I find these make me feel too edgy and I end up crashing afterwards. I usually have a shot of coffee instead.

WORKOUTS:

GET THEM DONE IN 20

BOOM!

Six different workouts to be completed over 12 weeks – easy! With the time spent in the active phase of each workout getting progressively longer as you go, it's more than challenging enough for 12 weeks and you will be amazed at your physical transformation.

All workouts will take 20 minutes to complete and are made up of four 5-minute sets. Each set consists of five different exercises, which you do for 1 minute each (including the rest time). Do as many repetitions of the exercise as you can in the time allocated, making sure to keep good form.

You will need to do each workout once per week, totalling three workouts per week on alternate days; however, if you want to train more often you can complete each workout twice a week, totalling six workouts per week. If you do choose to train more often, you must make sure to have at least one rest day per week.

12-WEEK PLAN

WEEKS 1 & 2

Complete workouts 1a, 1b and 1c. Work each exercise in turn for 20 seconds, then rest for 40 seconds. Repeat three more times for a total of four sets (20 minutes total).

WEEKS 3 & 4

Complete workouts 2a, 2b and 2c. Work 20 seconds/rest 40 seconds. Repeat three more times for a total of four sets (20 minutes total).

WEEKS 5 & 6

Complete workouts 1a, 1b and 1c. Work 30 seconds/rest 30 seconds. Repeat three more times for a total of four sets (20 minutes total).

WEEKS 7 & 8

Complete workouts 2a, 2b and 2c. Work 30 seconds/rest 30 seconds. Repeat three more times for a total of four sets (20 minutes total).

WEEKS 9 & 10

Complete workouts 1a, 1b and 1c. Work 40 seconds/rest 20 seconds. Repeat three more times for a total of four sets (20 minutes total).

WEEKS 11 & 12

Complete workouts 2a, 2b and 2c. Work 40 seconds/rest 20 seconds. Repeat three more times for a total of four sets (20 minutes total).

WORKOUT 1A

Complete the circuit four times.

Weeks 1 & 2: Work 20 seconds/rest 40 seconds
Weeks 5 & 6: Work 30 seconds/rest 30 seconds
Weeks 9 & 10: Work 40 seconds/rest 20 seconds

SQUATS

STAND with your feet shoulder-width apart. Keep your chest up and shoulders back.

BEND your knees and lower your butt backwards as if you are sitting on a chair.

RETURN to standing. Always keep the weight on your heels and your back straight. Repeat for the specified time.

MOUNTAIN CLIMBERS

START in push-up position. Keep your shoulders back. Keep your abdominal muscles (abs) pulled in and your body straight. Squeeze your glutes (butt muscles) and pull your shoulders away from your ears.

PULL the knees in right, left, right, left – switching simultaneously as if you are running. Repeat for the specified time.

FORWARD LUNGES

STEP forward with one leg and lower your back knee as close to the ground as you can without touching.

KEEP the weight on your heels as you push off your front foot and return to standing. Repeat with the other leg and alternate for the specified time.

RUNNING ON THE SPOT

KEEPING the weight on your toes, your back straight and core engaged, run on the spot.

LIFT your knees high, keep your head up and pump your arms. Continue for the specified time.

ABS BICYCLE

LIE on your back in sit-up position with your shoulders off the ground and fingertips on temples.

BEND your legs to 90 degrees and alternately bring your knees in to meet the opposite elbow.

CONTINUE alternating as if you are riding a bicycle for the specified time.

Increase fat loss by performing exercises at a higher intensity.

WORKOUT 1B

Complete the circuit four times.

Weeks 1 & 2: Work 20 seconds/rest 40 seconds
Weeks 5 & 6: Work 30 seconds/rest 30 seconds
Weeks 9 & 10: Work 40 seconds/rest 20 seconds

ICE SKATERS

BEGIN in a standing position with your feet shoulder-width apart. Look forward and keep your chest up. Keep your knees and hips soft and your back straight.

STEP your right foot back behind the left foot. In the same motion, reach down and touch the ground in front of your left foot with your right hand.

RETURN to a standing position and repeat the same movement on the opposite side. Continue to alternate for the specified time.

BURPEES

STAND with your feet shoulder-width apart. Keep your weight on your heels and your arms at your sides.

PUSH your hips back, bend your knees and lower your body into a squat.

PLACE your hands on the floor directly in front of your feet.

SHIFT your weight onto your hands, then jump your feet back and do a push-up.

JUMP your feet forward so that they land just behind your hands and come into a squat.

REACH your arms over your head as you jump up into the air.

LAND softly and repeat for the specified time.

Push-ups can be done on your knees instead,

depending on your skill level (see page 52).

REVERSE LUNGES

STAND with your feet shoulder-width apart.

STEP one foot back and lower your back knee to the ground. Keep your back straight and core engaged. Do not allow your front knee to bend past the line of your toe.

KEEP the weight on your heels as you push off your back foot and return to standing. Repeat on the opposite leg and continue for the specified time.

PUSH-UPS

START with your hands on the floor and in line with your shoulders, and your toes (or knees) on the ground. Keep your body in a straight line from shoulders to toes (or knees).

BEND your elbows outward until your chest is approximately 10 cm off the floor.

KEEP your core engaged and push through your arms, returning to the start position. Repeat for the specified time.

PLANK

START with your hands and knees on the ground. Keep your shoulders directly over your hands. Keep your abs pulled in and your body straight.

BRACE your core to make sure you are in a strong position before straightening your knees and taking the weight onto your toes. Keep your knees straight, core engaged and focus on contracting your abs. Hold for the specified time.

WORKOUT 1C

Complete the circuit four times.

Weeks 1 & 2: Work 20 seconds/rest 40 seconds
Weeks 5 & 6: Work 30 seconds/rest 30 seconds
Weeks 9 & 10: Work 40 seconds/rest 20 seconds

BEAR CRAWL

START by kneeling on all fours and lift your knees just off the ground.

KEEPING your spine in a neutral position and your head looking at the ground, crawl forward four steps, then crawl backwards four steps.

REPEAT for the specified time.

JUMPING JACKS

WITH your arms by your sides, plant both feet together on the floor.

QUICKLY jump both feet outwards so that they are spread slightly further than your hips. At the same time, raise your arms upwards and outwards from the sides of your body so that your hands almost meet directly above your head.

QUICKLY jump both of your feet inwards to bring them back together while lowering your arms downwards and in towards your body to return to starting position.

REPEAT for the specified time.

YOGA PUSH-UPS

START in push-up position with your feet a little wider than hip-width apart. Keep your core engaged and your back flat.

PUSH your torso backwards and raise your butt up to move into a pike position so your body forms an inverted V.

USING a smooth movement, bend your elbows to lower your upper chest to the ground while keeping your butt up. As you

lower your chest, drop your butt down so your body is in a straight line when you're closest to the ground.

STRAIGHTEN your arms to push your chest up, but allow for a slight arch in your back.

FROM this position, push your torso backwards and repeat the sequence. Continue for the specified time.

JUMPING SQUATS

STAND with your feet shoulder-width apart. Look forward and keep your chest up.

KEEP your chest up and shoulders back. Keep the weight on your heels and your back straight at all times as you bend your knees and lower your butt backwards as if you are sitting on a chair.

JUMP up into the air and land softly.

REPEAT for the specified time.

CRUNCHES

LIE flat on your back with your knees bent. Keep your feet together or cross them over.

PLACE your fingers on your temples and use your abs to bring your chest up off the ground and lower back down. Contract your abs with every repetition. Continue for the specified time.

Yoga push-ups can be done on your knees instead, depending on your skill level (see page 56).

WORKOUT 2A

Complete the circuit four times.

Weeks 3 & 4: Work 20 seconds/rest 40 seconds
Weeks 7 & 8: Work 30 seconds/rest 30 seconds
Weeks 11 & 12: Work 40 seconds/rest 20 seconds

···· SQUATS ····

STAND with your feet shoulder-width apart. Keep your chest up and shoulders back.

BEND your knees and lower your butt backwards as if you are sitting on a chair.

RETURN to standing. Keep the weight on your heels and your back straight at all times. Repeat for the specified time.

···· PUSH-UPS ····

START with your hands on the floor and in line with your shoulders, and your toes (or knees) on the ground. Keep your body in a straight line from shoulders to toes (or knees).

BEND your elbows outward until your chest is approximately 10 cm off the floor.

KEEP your core engaged and push through your arms, returning to the start position. Repeat for the specified time.

Push-ups can be done on your knees
(as pictured here), depending on your skill level.
For the advanced version, see page 49.

ICE SKATERS

BEGIN in a standing position with your feet shoulder-width apart. Look forward and keep your chest up. Keep your knees and hips soft and your back straight.

STEP your right foot back behind the left foot. In the same motion, reach down and touch the ground in front of your left foot with your right hand.

RETURN to a standing position and repeat the same movement on the opposite side. Continue to alternate for the specified time.

BEAR CRAWL

START by kneeling on all fours with your knees just off the ground.

KEEPING your spine in a neutral position and your head looking at the ground, crawl forward four steps, then crawl backwards four steps.

REPEAT for the specified time.

RUSSIAN TWIST

LIE down on the floor with your legs straight.

ELEVATE your upper body to about 60 degrees off the ground and bend your knees. Your arms should be fully extended in front of you with your fingers touching.

ENGAGE your abs and twist your torso to the right side until your arms are parallel with the floor.

HOLD for a second and move back to the starting position before rotating to the left side.

REPEAT for the specified time.

WORKOUT 2B

Complete the circuit four times.

Weeks 3 & 4: Work 20 seconds/rest 40 seconds
Weeks 7 & 8: Work 30 seconds/rest 30 seconds
Weeks 11 & 12: Work 40 seconds/rest 20 seconds

JUMPING LUNGES

JUMP forward with one leg and lower your back knee as close to the ground as you can without touching. Keep your back straight and core engaged. Do not allow your front knee to bend past the line of your toe.

KEEP the weight on your heels as you push off your front foot and jump to change your feet and land softly on your toes, sinking into a lunge on the opposite side.

REPEAT for the specified time.

BURPEES

STAND with your feet shoulder-width apart. Keep your weight on your heels and your arms at your sides.

PUSH your hips back, bend your knees, lower your body into a squat and place your hands on the floor directly in front of your feet.

SHIFT your weight onto your hands, jump your feet back and do a push-up.

JUMP your feet forward so that they land just behind your hands.

REACH your arms over your head as you jump up into the air.

LAND softly and repeat for the specified time.

Add another cycle if you feel you can push it harder!

JUMPING JACKS

WITH your arms by your sides, plant both feet together on the floor. **QUICKLY** jump both feet outwards so that they are spread slightly further than your hips. At the same time, raise your arms upwards and outwards from the sides of your body so that your hands almost meet directly above your head.

QUICKLY jump both of your feet inwards to bring them back together while lowering your arms downwards and in towards your body to return to starting position. **REPEAT** for the specified time.

RUNNING ON THE SPOT

KEEPING the weight on your toes, your back straight and core engaged, run on the spot.

LIFT your knees high, keep your head up and pump your arms. Continue for the specified time.

JACKKNIFE

LIE flat on your back with your arms extended straight back behind your head and your legs extended, slightly off the floor.

BEND at the waist and raise your legs and arms simultaneously to meet your feet. Your back should be off the floor and your arms and legs as straight as possible.

LOWER your arms and legs back to the starting position. Repeat for the specified time.

WORKOUT 2C

Complete the circuit four times.

Weeks 3 & 4: Work 20 seconds/rest 40 seconds
Weeks 7 & 8: Work 30 seconds/rest 30 seconds
Weeks 11 & 12: Work 40 seconds/rest 20 seconds

MOUNTAIN CLIMBERS

START in push-up position. Keep your shoulders back, abs pulled in and body straight. Squeeze your glutes and pull your shoulders away from your ears.

PULL the knees in right, left, right, left – switching simultaneously as if you are running.

REPEAT for the specified time.

REVERSE LUNGES

STAND with your feet shoulder-width apart. Look forward and keep your chest up.

STEP one foot back and lower your back knee to the ground. Keep your back straight and core engaged. Do not allow your front knee to bend past the line of your toe.

KEEP the weight on your heels as you push off your back foot and return to standing.

REPEAT on the opposite side and continue to alternate for the specified time.

YOGA PUSH-UPS

START in push-up position with your feet a little wider than hip-width apart. Keep your core engaged and your back flat.

PUSH your torso backwards and raise your butt up to move into a pike position so your body forms an inverted V.

USING a smooth movement, bend your elbows to lower your upper chest to the ground while keeping your butt up. As you lower your chest, drop your butt down so your body is in a straight line when you're closest to the ground.

STRAIGHTEN your arms to push your chest up, but allow for a slight arch in your back.

FROM this position, push your torso backwards and repeat the sequence. Continue for the specified time.

BURPEES

STAND with your feet shoulder-width apart. Keep your weight in your heels and your arms at your sides.

PUSH your hips back, bend your knees and lower your body into a squat.

PLACE your hands on the floor directly in front of your feet.

SHIFT your weight onto your hands, jump your feet back into a plank, then do a push-up.

JUMP your feet forwards so that they land just behind your hands and come into a squat.

REACH your arms over your head as you jump up into the air.

LAND softly and repeat for the specified time.

V CRUNCHES

SIT on the floor with your elbows bent and lift your legs up straight so they are extended towards the ceiling.

WITHOUT letting them touch the ground, lower your legs towards the floor. If it's too difficult to do with your legs straight, bend your knees slightly. Repeat for the specified time.

Yoga push-ups can be done on your knees

(as pictured here), depending on your skill level.

For the advanced version, see page 50.

RECIPES:

ON THE TABLE IN 30

DONE!

BREAKFAST
FIX

CORE MEALS //

POST-WORKOUT MEALS //

TROPICAL PAPAYA FRUIT SALAD

PREP: **8 MINUTES** // SERVES: **2** // Ⓥ

**250 g (1 cup) cottage cheese or
    Greek yoghurt; for extra protein,
    add 1 scoop (2 tablespoons)
    protein powder**
pinch of ground cinnamon
260 g (2 cups) mixed fresh berries
2 tablespoons olive oil or flaxseed oil
1 papaya, halved and seeds removed
2 tablespoons maple syrup or honey
1 orange, halved
6 mint leaves

Place the cottage cheese or yoghurt and protein powder (if using) in a small bowl and add the cinnamon, mixing well. Place the berries in another bowl and drizzle with the olive or flaxseed oil. Mix well.

Spoon half the cottage cheese or yoghurt mixture into the hollow of each papaya half, then divide the berries between the two. Drizzle the maple syrup or honey over the berries and squeeze the orange halves over everything. Add the mint leaves and enjoy.

EASY!

ZESTY PEAR & GRAPEFRUIT SALAD

PREP: **8 MINUTES** // SERVES: **2** // Ⓥ

1 large firm pear
1 large grapefruit
125 g (½ cup) Greek yoghurt or
    coconut yoghurt
zest of 1 lime
3 tablespoons hazelnuts, toasted
3 tablespoons pomegranate seeds
2 tablespoons maple syrup or honey
1 small handful of mint leaves

Cut the pear into large pieces and peel and segment the grapefruit, removing any seeds.

Divide the yoghurt between two bowls.

Divide the fruit pieces equally between the bowls and add the lime zest to taste. Scatter the hazelnuts and pomegranate seeds over and finish with a drizzle of maple syrup or honey and a sprinkle of mint leaves.

*Tip:
I like to use Bosc
or Anjou pears for
this dish.*

KEFIR BREAKFAST BOWL
WITH BERRIES
& CARAMELISED PAPAYA

PREP: **5 MINUTES** // COOK: **10 MINUTES** // SERVES: **2** // (V)

½ small papaya, cut into bite-sized cubes
155 g (1 cup) fresh blueberries
1 tablespoon maple syrup or honey
finely grated zest and juice of 1 orange
2 pinches of sea salt
375 ml (1½ cups) kefir
2 tablespoons hazelnuts, toasted
3 tablespoons pumpkin seeds, toasted
1 tablespoon sesame seeds, toasted
4 mint sprigs, leaves picked

Heat a non-stick frying pan over medium–high heat. Carefully add the papaya cubes and let the heat caramelise the natural sugar, being careful not to burn the papaya too much. The sweetness will intensify while cooking. Move the cubes around a little for 3–4 minutes, or until they are nicely caramelised on all sides. Remove from the heat and transfer to a plate.

Wipe the pan and return it to the heat. Add the blueberries, maple syrup or honey, orange zest and juice and salt. Stir and let the juice reduce a bit while the berries warm up.

Pour the kefir into two bowls. Divide the caramelised papaya between the bowls. Remove the blueberries from the heat and stir gently. Pour directly over the papaya and top with the toasted nuts and seeds and mint.

Tip: Kefir is a fermented milk drink. You can buy it at most health-food stores or make it yourself.

PROTEIN POWERHOUSE
PARFAIT – *BOOM!*

PREP: **8 MINUTES** // SERVES: **2** // Ⓥ

250 g (1 cup) Greek yoghurt
2 scoops (4 tablespoons) protein
powder of your choice
155 g (1 cup) fresh blueberries
125 g (1 cup) fresh raspberries
2 tablespoons sunflower seeds
2 tablespoons pumpkin seeds
30 g (½ cup) shredded coconut, toasted
2 tablespoons honey or maple syrup

Place the yoghurt in a large bowl and add the protein powder. Mix with a wire whisk to make sure that the powder is properly blended. Depending on the consistency of the yoghurt, it might thicken when the protein powder is added; if this happens, simply add a little water and continue whisking to the desired consistency.

Scoop the yoghurt mixture into two breakfast bowls and add the berries, seeds and coconut. Finish by drizzling with the honey or maple syrup.

Tip:
Change up the berries and seeds used here to make this dish your own!

CHARRED STRAWBERRIES
with YOGHURT & MUESLI

PREP: **10 MINUTES** // COOK: **10 MINUTES** // SERVES: **2** // Ⓥ

coconut oil
300 g (2 cups) large strawberries,
    cut in half
1 tablespoon maple syrup or honey
80 g (½ cup) almonds, toasted
125 g (1 cup) ready-made muesli
70 g (½ cup) mixed sunflower, sesame
    and pumpkin seeds
2 tablespoons bee pollen
375 g (1½ cups) plain yoghurt
10 basil leaves
olive oil, to serve

Coat a non-stick frying pan with a small amount of coconut oil and heat over high heat. Place the strawberries, cut-side down, in the pan and leave them until they get a nice charred look. Do this in batches to get all the pieces equally charred. This will bring out a lovely sweetness.

Divide the strawberries between two serving bowls, drizzle over the maple syrup or honey and scatter the almonds, muesli and seeds over the top, followed by the bee pollen. Finish with dollops of the yoghurt, basil leaves and a drizzle of olive oil.

DONE!

Tip:
High in protein and nutrients, bee pollen can be bought at most health-food stores.

CORE MEAL

CHEESY SCRAMBLE
WITH GREENS

PREP: **8 MINUTES** // COOK: **6 MINUTES** // SERVES: **2** // Ⓥ

6 eggs
2 tablespoons olive oil
1 tablespoon milk (optional)
45 g goat's cheese, crumbled
1 tablespoon chopped chives or
   spring onion (green part)
1 tablespoon chopped dill fronds
6 basil leaves
90 g (2 cups) rocket leaves
2 tablespoons extra-virgin olive oil
red wine vinegar, to taste
sea salt and freshly ground
   black pepper

Heat a non-stick frying pan over medium heat.

In a bowl, beat the eggs with 1 tablespoon of the olive oil or milk until frothy and blended. Stir the goat's cheese and herbs through the egg mixture.

Lightly coat the hot pan with the remaining olive oil. Add the egg and quickly cook until a soft scramble forms, being careful not to overcook. Set aside.

Place the rocket in a bowl. Drizzle with the extra-virgin olive oil and add a few drops of red wine vinegar and salt and pepper to taste. Divide the rocket between two serving bowls.

Divide the scramble between the serving bowls and enjoy warm.

Tip:
Serve with
a piece of toasted
wholegrain bread
if you desire.

CRUNCHY BREAKFAST SALAD
WITH SOFT-BOILED EGGS

PREP: **10 MINUTES** // COOK: **8 MINUTES** // SERVES: **2** // Ⓥ

1 small red onion, finely sliced
3 tablespoons olive oil, plus
   1 tablespoon extra to serve
1 tablespoon red wine vinegar
1 tablespoon maple syrup
sea salt
4 eggs
1 avocado, diced
1 large continental cucumber,
   peeled and chopped
3 tomatoes, chopped
½ cup equal parts chopped basil,
   dill and mint leaves

Bring a small saucepan of water to the boil.

Meanwhile, soak the onion in iced water for 5 minutes to reduce the strong, raw flavour.

Mix the olive oil, vinegar and maple syrup together with a little salt and set aside.

Use a spoon to gently place each egg in the boiling water and set a timer for 6½ minutes. When the eggs are done, use a slotted spoon to transfer them to a bowl of iced water. When cool enough to handle, carefully peel the eggs, cut them in half and set aside to cool.

Remove the onion from the water and pat dry. In a bowl, mix the onion, avocado, cucumber and tomato together with the prepared dressing. Divide the salad between two serving bowls and add two egg halves to each. Drizzle the remaining olive oil over the eggs and scatter the herbs on top.

ENJOY!

SPICY SAUSAGE OMELETTE WITH 'SHROOMS & GREENS

PREP: 10 MINUTES // COOK: 18 MINUTES // SERVES: 2

2 tablespoons olive oil or grapeseed oil
½ cup chopped shiitake mushrooms or
   button mushrooms
80 g (2 cups) roughly chopped
   English spinach leaves
sea salt and freshly ground
   black pepper
2 large (or 4 small) spicy lamb sausages
6 eggs (or 8 egg whites if you prefer)
2 handfuls of green salad leaves
2 tablespoons chopped basil leaves
juice of ½ lemon or 1 tablespoon
   red wine vinegar
2 tablespoons extra-virgin olive oil

*Tip:
You can use
any organic
sausages you
like here.*

Heat a large frying pan over medium heat. When the pan is hot, drizzle in 2 teaspoons of the olive or grapeseed oil and add the chopped mushrooms. Sauté for 2–3 minutes, or until golden, then add the spinach. The spinach will cook quickly, in about 1 minute, due to its high water content. When the spinach is wilted and the mushrooms are caramelised, season with salt and pepper and transfer the mixture to a small bowl.

Return the pan to the heat and increase to medium–high. Split the sausages lengthways down the middle to open slightly and drizzle 2 teaspoons of the oil into the pan. Add the split sausages with the cut-sides down and press. This will help the sausages cook faster. Depending on the size of the sausages, cook for 3–5 minutes on each side, or until golden and firm to the touch.

Meanwhile, mix the eggs or egg whites with a fork or whisk. Coat another small frying pan with the remaining olive or grapeseed oil and heat over medium heat. When the oil is hot, pour the egg into the pan and stir vigorously, then flatten out the mixture. Once the underside is set, after about 3 minutes, add the mushroom and spinach mixture on one half of the omelette. With a spatula, lift the opposite half of the omelette and fold it over the mixture. After 1 minute, you should be able to flip the entire omelette onto the other side. Turn off the heat and leave in the pan for another minute. Remove the sausages from the heat and drain on paper towel.

To serve, divide the omelette in two and serve with a sausage (or two) on each plate. Season with salt and pepper to taste. Combine the salad leaves and basil and toss with the lemon juice or vinegar and extra-virgin olive oil, then divide between the serving plates.

HEARTY BREAKFAST BOWL

PREP: **8 MINUTES** // COOK: **10 MINUTES** // SERVES: **2** // Ⓥ

250 ml (1 cup) vegetable stock or water
100 g (½ cup) quinoa, rinsed
75 g (1 cup) shredded red or
 white cabbage
4 large mint leaves
4 large basil leaves
1 tomato, roughly diced
40 g (1 cup) finely sliced kale leaves
1 tablespoon apple cider vinegar
2 teaspoons maple syrup or honey
3 tablespoons olive oil
sea salt and freshly ground
 black pepper
1½ tablespoons white vinegar
2 eggs
1 large avocado, peeled, halved
 and destoned

Place the stock or water in a saucepan and bring to the boil. Add the quinoa and lower the heat to medium. Cover and cook for 10 minutes, then set aside, still covered.

Meanwhile, fill another saucepan with enough water to come three-quarters of the way up the side. Bring to the boil.

In a large bowl, combine the cabbage, herbs, tomato, kale, apple cider vinegar and maple syrup or honey with 2 tablespoons of the olive oil. Season with salt and pepper to taste and mix well.

Lower the heat for the saucepan of boiling water to a simmer and add the white vinegar and a pinch of salt. Swirl to make a whirlpool, then crack each egg individually into a coffee cup or ramekin and gently pour into the centre of the whirlpool. Remove the eggs after 2–3 minutes and transfer to a bowl of cold water to stop the cooking process.

Divide the quinoa between two bowls and place half the salad on top of each. Top each bowl with a poached egg and an avocado half, then drizzle with the remaining olive oil to finish.

*Tip:
Massaging
the sliced kale in
1 teaspoon of olive
oil before mixing it
with the rest of the
ingredients can help
to soften it up.*

WILD MUSHROOM FRITTATA – *YUM!*

PREP: **10 MINUTES** // COOK: **13 MINUTES** // SERVES: **2** // (V)

2 tablespoons extra-virgin olive oil
1 cup mixed mushrooms, sliced
1 large leek, white part only, washed and sliced
1 garlic clove, finely chopped
90 g (2 cups) baby spinach leaves
6 eggs
30 g (¼ cup) crumbled feta or goat's cheese
1 small handful of rocket leaves

In a non-stick frying pan over medium heat, heat 1 tablespoon of the olive oil and add the mushroom, leek and garlic. Keep moving them around the pan until translucent and slightly golden, without burning, then add the spinach and move it around until it is wilted.

Crack the eggs into a bowl and whisk briskly until frothy. Add the crumbled cheese to the eggs and pour into the mushroom mixture, stirring to combine. Lower the heat to medium–low and cover with a lid to speed up the cooking.

After about 6 minutes, uncover and shake the pan around to see if the frittata is ready. The sides should lift easily and the centre should still be slightly soft and a little raw. Turn off the heat and leave it in the hot pan for another 5 minutes.

Place a plate over the pan and flip over to release the frittata. Slice in half and divide between two plates. Scatter over the rocket, drizzle with the remaining olive oil and serve.

SUPER GREENS & EGGS ON TOAST FOR TWO LUCKY PEOPLE

PREP: **10 MINUTES** // COOK: **10 MINUTES** // SERVES: **2** // ⓥ

4 eggs
1 small French shallot, finely chopped
¼ cup marinated red capsicum,
  drained and finely chopped
2 tablespoons extra-virgin olive oil
2 pinches of smoked paprika
1 tablespoon red wine vinegar
3 tablespoons red hot sauce
  of your choice
2 teaspoons maple syrup or honey
sea salt
1 thin slice of wholemeal bread,
  cut into small cubes
40 g (1 cup) roughly chopped
  kale leaves
1 large avocado, peeled, halved
  and destoned
1 tablespoon sesame seeds, toasted

Bring a saucepan of water to the boil and use a spoon to carefully lower the eggs in one at a time. Cook for exactly 6 ½ minutes. Prepare a bowl of iced water that will hold the eggs, then remove the cooked eggs from the boiling water and place them in the iced water.

While the eggs chill, combine the shallot, capsicum, 1 tablespoon of the olive oil, the paprika, vinegar, hot sauce and maple syrup or honey in a bowl and mix well. Set aside.

In a small frying pan over medium heat, heat 2 teaspoons of the olive oil and a pinch of salt, then add the cubes of bread. Fry the bread until crispy on all sides, then set aside.

In the same pan, add the remaining olive oil, the kale and a pinch of salt and quickly move around to just wilt the kale while getting some crispy edges.

Peel the eggs and place two on each plate. Crush them with the back of a fork and spread them out slightly. Top with the hot sauce mixture, followed by the wilted kale, croutons, an avocado half and the sesame seeds.

CHEESY PUMPKIN & SPINACH OMELETTE

PREP: **5 MINUTES** // COOK: **7 MINUTES** // SERVES: **2** // Ⓥ

150 g butternut pumpkin, finely diced
6 eggs
sea salt and freshly ground
   black pepper
1 tablespoon extra-virgin olive oil,
   plus extra for drizzling
90 g (2 cups) baby spinach leaves
50 g (½ cup) finely grated pecorino
90 g (2 cups) rocket leaves
juice of ½ lemon
2 large roasted macadamia nuts

Bring a small saucepan of water to the boil, add the pumpkin and cook for 3–4 minutes, or until it is fork tender but not mushy. Drain and set aside.

In a bowl, whisk the eggs with some salt and pepper. Place a non-stick frying pan over medium–low heat, then add the olive oil and spinach. Once the spinach has wilted and some of the water has evaporated, add the eggs and move them around in a circular motion. Once the side starts lifting from the pan, spread the cooked pumpkin evenly over one half of the omelette. Scatter the grated pecorino over the pumpkin and carefully flip the other side of the omelette over with a spatula to cover the pumpkin. Cover with a lid and cook for 2 minutes.

Remove the pan from the heat and slide the omelette onto a large plate. Cut in half to make two servings.

In a separate bowl, combine the rocket, lemon juice, a couple of pinches of salt and a light drizzle of olive oil. Place the omelette halves on plates and top with the rocket mixture. Finish by grating the macadamias over both plates.

EASY!

CORE MEAL

BLACK BEAN, QUINOA & CAPSICUM SALAD WITH FRIED EGGS

PREP: **8 MINUTES** // COOK: **12 MINUTES** // SERVES: **2** // Ⓥ

2 tablespoons olive oil, plus extra
   for drizzling
1 red capsicum, deseeded and sliced
1 green capsicum, deseeded and sliced
1 yellow capsicum, deseeded and sliced
½ large onion, finely chopped
1 teaspoon ground cumin
1 teaspoon smoked paprika
sea salt and freshly ground
   black pepper
1 x 425 g can black beans, drained,
   rinsed and dried
185 g (1 cup) cooked quinoa
1½ tablespoons red wine vinegar
2 teaspoons maple syrup or honey
2 eggs
1 small handful of basil leaves
2 coriander sprigs, leaves picked

Heat 1 tablespoon of the olive oil in a frying pan over medium heat. Add the capsicum, onion, cumin and paprika, then season with salt and pepper. Cook for 3–5 minutes, or until softened and caramelised, then add the black beans and quinoa to warm through. Transfer to a bowl and drizzle with some extra olive oil, the red wine vinegar and maple syrup or honey. Season with salt and pepper to taste.

Fry the eggs in a non-stick frying pan over medium–high heat with 1 tablespoon of olive oil until cooked to your liking.

Meanwhile, add the basil and coriander leaves to the bean and quinoa mixture, mixing well. Divide the mixture between two bowls and top each one with a fried egg. Season to taste.

*Tip:
You can buy pre-cooked and microwaveable quinoa in most supermarkets. I like to add extra herbs and a drizzle of olive oil to finish.*

GARLICKY SILVERBEET
WITH **CHILLI, AVO & EGGS**

PREP: **8 MINUTES** // COOK: **12 MINUTES** // SERVES: **2** // (V)

80 ml (⅓ cup) olive oil
2 garlic cloves, finely sliced
190 g silverbeet, central stems removed
  and leaves roughly chopped
1 teaspoon chilli flakes
2 tablespoons red wine vinegar
sea salt
4 eggs
1 avocado, diced
1 red chilli, deseeded and finely sliced
freshly ground black pepper
parmesan, for shaving (optional)
1 small handful of flat-leaf parsley
  leaves, to serve

Heat a large non-stick frying pan over medium heat and add 1 tablespoon of the olive oil along with the garlic. Lightly sauté for 1–2 minutes, or until soft and translucent.

Add the silverbeet and 2 tablespoons of the olive oil to the pan and sauté until the leaves wilt and mix with the garlic. Add the chilli flakes, 1 tablespoon of the red wine vinegar and a pinch of salt and sauté for a further 5 minutes.

Spread the silverbeet evenly in the pan and make four even holes. Crack an egg into each hole. Add the avocado, cover and cook for 5–7 minutes, or until the eggs are slightly set but not firm.

Remove the lid, scatter with the sliced chilli and season with more salt, some pepper and the remaining olive oil and red wine vinegar. Divide between two plates and serve with the shaved parmesan (if using) and parsley.

PERFECT POACHED EGGS
WITH SMOKED SALMON
& BARLEY – *DELISH!*

PREP: **8 MINUTES** // COOK: **3 MINUTES** // SERVES: **2**

1½ tablespoons white vinegar

sea salt

4 eggs

2 tablespoons chopped flat-leaf
  parsley leaves

2 tablespoons chopped chives

2 tablespoons chopped mint leaves

2 tablespoons olive oil

3½ cups cooked barley (see Note)

½ lemon

freshly ground black pepper

90 g (2 cups) rocket or spinach leaves

100 g smoked salmon

2 tablespoons crème fraîche

Half fill a small saucepan with water and bring to a simmer. Add the vinegar and a large pinch of salt and swirl to make a whirlpool. Crack each egg individually into a coffee cup or ramekin and gently pour into the centre of the whirlpool. Remove after 2–3 minutes and transfer to a bowl of cold water to stop the cooking process.

Combine the chopped herbs in a bowl with half the olive oil and season with salt. Add the cooked barley to the herb mixture with a squeeze of lemon juice and some freshly ground pepper. Spoon onto two plates.

Remove the poached eggs from the cold water and place two on top of the barley mixture, along with the rocket or spinach. Drizzle with the remaining olive oil and add a sprinkle of salt.

Divide the smoked salmon between the plates and serve with a dollop of crème fraîche.

Note: To cook the barley, bring 500 ml (2 cups) of water and 220 g (1 cup) of barley to the boil and cook for 20–30 minutes, until tender. Drain and set aside to cool. Barley will always have a bit of texture no matter how long you cook it for. This is due to the fibre and proteins the grain naturally contains.

CREAMY BANANA
PORRIDGE

PREP: **10 MINUTES** // COOK: **8 MINUTES** // SERVES: **2** // Ⓥ

375 ml (1½ cups) water or milk
100 g (1 cup) rolled oats
pinch of ground cinnamon
pinch of sea salt
1 tablespoon butter or olive oil
2 scoops (4 tablespoons) protein
   powder of your choice
2 tablespoons maple syrup
1 large banana, sliced
45 g (¼ cup) pitted and halved dates
2 tablespoons dehydrated buckwheat,
   sunflower seeds or flaxseeds
70 g (½ cup) hazelnuts, toasted and
   roughly chopped

In a saucepan over medium–low heat, heat the water or milk until simmering. Add the oats, cinnamon, salt and butter or olive oil. Stir constantly until the mixture becomes creamy (add a little extra water or milk if it is too thick). Add the protein powder slowly so it doesn't clump up, whisking quickly, then add the maple syrup. After 6 minutes, the porridge should be done.

Pour the porridge into two bowls and divide the banana, dates, buckwheat or seeds and hazelnuts between the two.

Tip:
Season with sea salt and enjoy with extra maple syrup if you like.

SPICED ANCIENT GRAIN
PORRIDGE – *ENJOY!*

PREP: **8 MINUTES** // COOK: **10 MINUTES** // SERVES: **2** // Ⓥ

½ teaspoon ground cinnamon

¼ teaspoon ground ginger

250 ml (1 cup) almond milk, coconut milk or milk of your choice

½ cup amaranth seeds, soaked in water overnight (see Tip), then drained

1 tablespoon olive oil

2 tablespoons maple syrup or honey, plus extra to serve

80 g (½ cup) almonds, toasted

1 tablespoon coconut oil

1 large red apple, skin on, cored and cut into chunks

2 tablespoons Greek yoghurt

¼ teaspoon sea salt

Place 125 ml (½ cup) of water in a saucepan with the spices and milk, then add the amaranth. Bring to the boil, then turn the heat to low and simmer with the lid on for 10 minutes, stirring occasionally to prevent sticking, until the amaranth mixture reaches the consistency of porridge. Add the olive oil and 1 tablespoon of the maple syrup or honey, along with the toasted almonds.

Meanwhile, heat a frying pan over medium heat and add the coconut oil, apple and the remaining maple syrup or honey. Cook for 4–6 minutes, or until the apple becomes soft and slightly browned. Remove from the heat and set aside.

Divide the porridge between two bowls. Top each bowl with the apple and a tablespoon of yoghurt. Drizzle with some extra maple syrup or honey and scatter over a few flakes of sea salt.

Tip:
Soaking amaranth the night before speeds up the cooking process. If using un-soaked amaranth, increase the cooking time to 30 minutes.

WILD BERRY PORRIDGE
WITH TOASTED HAZELNUTS

PREP: **8 MINUTES** // COOK: **8 MINUTES** // SERVES: **2** // Ⓥ

100 g (1 cup) rolled oats

125 g (1 cup) mixed berries
(fresh or frozen), plus a few extra
fresh berries to serve

pinch of ground cinnamon

500 ml (2 cups) milk or water,
plus extra if needed

1 tablespoon butter, ghee or
grapeseed oil

2 pinches of sea salt

3 tablespoons maple syrup or honey,
plus extra to serve

3 tablespoons toasted and chopped
hazelnuts

2 tablespoons Greek yoghurt

Combine the oats, mixed berries, cinnamon and milk or water in a small saucepan over medium heat. Cook for 7 minutes, stirring constantly, until the mixture is thick and creamy and the berries have released their juices. If necessary, add more milk or water to reach the desired consistency.

· ·

Add the butter, ghee or oil, salt and maple syrup or honey. Stir well and pour into two serving bowls. Add the hazelnuts, yoghurt, extra fresh berries and a drizzle of maple syrup or honey to finish.

· ·

DONE!

*Tip:
You can use
a coconut or other
non-dairy yoghurt
here if you
prefer.*

BANANA–BERRY
PANCAKES – *MY FAVE!*

PREP: **10 MINUTES** // COOK: **10 MINUTES** // SERVES: **2** // (V)

2 bananas
125 ml (½ cup) almond milk or
    any milk of your choice
2 eggs, lightly whisked
150 g (1 cup) spelt flour
1 teaspoon baking powder
½ teaspoon ground cinnamon
¼ teaspoon ground cardamom
½ teaspoon bicarbonate of soda
2 tablespoons ghee or light olive oil,
    plus extra if needed
125 ml (½ cup) maple syrup
195 g (1½ cups) mixed fresh berries
1 small handful of flaked coconut

Mash the bananas in a large bowl with a masher or the back of a fork. Add the milk, egg, spelt flour, baking powder, cinnamon, cardamom and bicarbonate of soda. Whisk until the mixture is smooth, with just a few lumps of banana. Set aside for about 3 minutes, or until some bubbles form. This will give the pancakes a nice fluffy texture.

Heat a non-stick frying pan over medium heat and lightly coat it with some of the ghee or oil. Pour about 3 tablespoons of batter per pancake into the pan. Cook the pancakes in batches of two or three for 1 minute on each side, or until golden, then transfer to a plate and cover to keep warm. Repeat until you have used up all of the batter. You should get six to eight pancakes.

Divide the pancakes between two plates. Warm up the maple syrup in a small saucepan and pour over the pancakes, adding some extra ghee or oil if you like. Top with the fresh berries and flaked coconut and enjoy.

SCRAMBLED EGG BREAKFAST QUESADILLA

PREP: 8 MINUTES // COOK: 10 MINUTES // SERVES: 2 // (V)

2 tablespoons olive oil
2 small tomatoes, finely diced
3 tablespoons finely chopped
  jalapeño chillies
½ white onion, finely chopped
2 tablespoons finely sliced spring onion
  (green part only)
4 eggs
45 g (½ cup) finely grated
  cheddar cheese
sea salt and freshly ground
  black pepper
2 large wholemeal tortillas
2 tablespoons finely chopped
  coriander leaves

Heat a large non-stick frying pan over medium heat and add 1 tablespoon of the olive oil, the tomato, jalapeño, onion and spring onion. Sauté for 3 minutes.

In a bowl, whisk the eggs together with the cheddar cheese and add salt and pepper to taste. Pour into the pan with the tomato mixture and add the remaining olive oil. Cook for 1–2 minutes, or until it starts coming together but is still creamy. Remove from the heat and set aside.

Heat a second large non-stick frying pan and toast a tortilla for 1–2 minutes. Add half the egg mixture and 1 tablespoon of the coriander and fold over the tortilla to make a half moon. Carefully flip onto the other side and toast for 1–2 minutes more. Repeat with the other tortilla and remaining egg mixture and coriander. Cut each tortilla in half and serve with your choice of accompaniments.

Tip:
I like to serve these with extra coriander leaves, sliced green chilli and a side of salsa.

BAKED MUSHROOMS & EGGS
ON SPELT TOAST

PREP: **6 MINUTES** // COOK: **20 MINUTES** // SERVES: **2** // Ⓥ

½ **large onion, finely diced**
2 tablespoons olive oil
1 tablespoon tomato paste
1 tablespoon red wine vinegar
2 teaspoons maple syrup or honey
**1 tablespoon soy sauce or tamari
    (gluten-free soy sauce)**
**sea salt and freshly ground
    black pepper**
2 large portobello mushrooms
4 eggs
80 g (2 cups) finely chopped kale leaves
2 slices of spelt bread
**finely grated pecorino or well-aged
    parmesan, to serve**

Preheat the oven to 180°C. Line a baking tray with baking paper.

Sauté the onion with 1 tablespoon of the olive oil in a frying pan over medium heat. Cook for 5 minutes, or until translucent, then add the tomato paste. Cook for 1 minute more and then add the red wine vinegar, maple syrup or honey, soy sauce or tamari and salt and pepper to taste. Cook for about 4 minutes, then remove from the heat.

Place the mushrooms on the prepared tray and top each with half of the onion mixture. Bake for 10 minutes.

Meanwhile, whisk the eggs until frothy. Add some salt and pepper.

Pour another tablespoon of olive oil into the same pan, add the kale and fry for 1 minute over medium–high heat. Add the egg and quickly cook until a soft scramble forms, being careful not to overcook.

Toast the bread until golden brown. Place the toast on two serving plates. Divide the scramble in half and place on top of each piece of toast. Finish with a baked mushroom and a sprinkle of cheese.

ENJOY!

SWEET POTATO
PANCAKES – *STACK 'EM!*

PREP: **10 MINUTES** // COOK: **10 MINUTES** // SERVES: **2** // (V)

1 large sweet potato, peeled
3 large eggs
50 g (½ cup) almond meal
2 teaspoons finely chopped
    rosemary leaves
1 teaspoon bicarbonate of soda
sea salt and freshly ground
    black pepper
1 tablespoon coconut oil
2 tablespoons olive oil
2 tablespoons maple syrup
4 mint sprigs, leaves picked

Use a large grater to coarsely grate the sweet potato. Place it in a blender along with 1 egg, the almond meal, rosemary, bicarbonate of soda and salt and pepper to taste and blend until smooth. Transfer to a bowl and set aside for 5 minutes.

Meanwhile, heat a non-stick frying pan over medium heat. Add some of the coconut oil and pour about 3 tablespoons of the sweet potato mixture per pancake into the pan, working in batches of two or three. You'll know it's time to flip the pancakes over when you shake the pan and the pancakes move: this generally takes about 2 minutes.

Gently flip the pancakes over and cook for another 1–2 minutes. Repeat with the remaining mixture. Keep the finished pancakes on a baking tray or plate and cover to keep warm.

Heat another frying pan over medium–high heat. Add the olive oil and crack the remaining eggs into the pan. Cover with a lid and cook for 2–3 minutes, or until the whites are cooked and the yolk is slightly firm but still runny. Remove from the pan and set aside.

Divide the pancakes between two plates and drizzle the maple syrup equally over both. Place one fried egg on each and finish with the mint and a sprinkle of salt.

VEGGIE-LOADED BREAKFAST TACOS

PREP: **8 MINUTES** // COOK: **10 MINUTES** // SERVES: **2** // Ⓥ

3 tablespoons light olive oil
1 onion, sliced
1 red capsicum, deseeded and sliced
45 g (1 cup) baby spinach leaves
1 lime
55 g (¾ cup) shredded red cabbage
4 eggs
4 corn tortillas
2 tablespoons sour cream
hot sauce, such as Tabasco (optional)

Heat 1 tablespoon of the olive oil in a frying pan over medium heat. Add the onion and capsicum and sauté for 2–3 minutes, or until soft and caramelised. Add the spinach and cook until just wilted. Remove from the heat and set aside in a bowl. Keep warm.

Finely grate the lime, then cut the lime in half, reserving one half for serving, and juice the other half. Combine the cabbage in a bowl with the lime zest and juice and toss to combine.

Heat another tablespoon of the olive oil in the frying pan over medium–low heat and fry the eggs, two at a time (or all at once if your pan is big enough). Cook slowly, without flipping, until the egg whites are opaque but the yolks are still runny.

Meanwhile, heat the tortillas over a flame or in a non-stick grill pan, so they are warm and soft. Divide the onion mixture among the tortillas, followed by the cabbage and the eggs. Dollop on the sour cream and squeeze the remaining lime juice over. Top with a little hot sauce, if using.

OAT PIZZA WITH ARTICHOKE & HAVARTI AKA PIZZA FOR BREKKIE!

PREP: **10 MINUTES** // COOK: **8 MINUTES** // SERVES: **2** // Ⓥ

100 g (1 cup) rolled oats
4 eggs
sea salt and freshly ground
   black pepper
½ cup chopped marinated artichoke
60 g (1 cup) chopped broccoli
40 g (1 cup) chopped English
   spinach leaves
2 tablespoons olive oil
125 ml (½ cup) tomato-based
   pasta sauce
½ cup shredded havarti cheese
2 teaspoons dried oregano

Preheat the oven to 190°C.

Mix the oats and 2 eggs in a small bowl, season with salt and pepper and set aside.

In another bowl, combine the artichoke, broccoli and English spinach. Mix well and set aside.

Heat a frying pan over medium–high heat and spray with cooking spray or use 1 tablespoon of the olive oil. Add the oat mixture and spread thinly to shape into a round pizza base. Cook for 1 minute on each side, then remove from the pan.

Spread the base with the pasta sauce. Spread half the shredded cheese over, followed by the mixed vegetables. Finish with the remaining cheese, then sprinkle with the oregano.

Crack the remaining eggs onto the pizza. Season with salt and drizzle with the remaining olive oil and bake for 6 minutes, or until the cheese is melting and the eggs are opaque but not overcooked. Cut into slices and enjoy.

FRIED EGGS
WITH CHARRED CORN
& BLACK BEANS

PREP: **10 MINUTES** // COOK: **7 MINUTES** // SERVES: **2** // Ⓥ

75 g (1 cup) shredded red cabbage
½ cup sugar snap peas
80 ml (⅓ cup) extra-virgin olive oil
100 g (½ cup) corn kernels, cut from fresh corncobs (or use frozen or canned corn kernels)
150 g (¾ cup) canned black beans, rinsed and drained
sea salt and freshly ground black pepper
½ cup fresh herbs, such as mint, basil and parsley leaves
2 eggs
2 tablespoons red wine vinegar
juice of ½ lemon
2 thick slices of sourdough or wholegrain bread, toasted
hot sauce, such as Tabasco (optional)

Soak the cabbage in a bowl of cold water.

Slice the sugar snap peas in half lengthways, then add them to the bowl of cold water with the cabbage.

Heat a frying pan over high heat, add 1 tablespoon of the olive oil and cook the corn and beans for 2–3 minutes, or until they get a little colour. Remove from the heat and season with salt and pepper and 1 tablespoon of the fresh herbs.

Heat a frying pan over medium heat and coat with a little of the olive oil. Break the eggs into the pan, season with salt, cover with a lid and cook for 1–2 minutes. Uncover the eggs and remove from the heat.

Drain the cabbage and peas and dry well. Dress the cabbage mix with 1 tablespoon of the olive oil, the red wine vinegar, lemon juice, salt and the remaining herb mixture. Place the toast on two serving plates. Divide the bean and corn mixture between the plates, top each with a fried egg and serve with the cabbage mixture alongside. Enjoy with some hot sauce (if using).

EASY
LUNCHES

CORE MEALS //

POST-WORKOUT MEALS //

HERBED PUMPKIN, FETA & RADISH ON RYE

PREP: **10 MINUTES** // COOK: **10 MINUTES** // SERVES: **2** // Ⓥ

225 g pumpkin, finely diced
4 slices of rye bread or any wholegrain
  bread of your choice
2 tablespoons chopped chives
2 teaspoons maple syrup or honey
sea salt and freshly ground
  black pepper
½ lemon
1 tablespoon extra-virgin olive oil
35 g (¼ cup) crumbled goat's feta
1 radish, finely sliced and briefly soaked
  in iced water
2 teaspoons sesame seeds, toasted

Bring a saucepan of water to the boil. Add the pumpkin and boil for 3–4 minutes, or until fork tender. Drain and set aside.

Toast the bread until golden and crisp.

In a bowl, combine the pumpkin, half the chives and 1 teaspoon of the maple syrup or honey. Season with salt and pepper and a squeeze of lemon. Drizzle over the olive oil and mash well using the back of a fork.

Spread the pumpkin mash over the pieces of toast and top with the crumbled feta, sliced radish, sesame seeds and the remaining chives. Finish with more salt, pepper and lemon juice to taste.

EASY!

SIMPLE VEGGIE
FRITTATA – *DONE!*

PREP: 8 MINUTES // COOK: 15 MINUTES // SERVES: 2 // Ⓥ

2 tablespoons olive oil
2 tomatoes, roughly chopped
65 g (¾ cup) diced button mushrooms
   or any mushroom of your choice
½ onion, diced
6 asparagus spears, woody ends
   trimmed, cut into 3 cm pieces
4 eggs
2 tablespoons milk
sea salt and freshly ground
   black pepper
60 g (½ cup) goat's cheese
2 tablespoons chopped chives
3 tablespoons finely chopped
   flat-leaf parsley leaves

Heat a non-stick frying pan over medium–high heat. Add the olive oil, tomato, mushroom, onion and asparagus. Sauté for 2–3 minutes, or until softened.

Whisk together the eggs and milk with a pinch of salt and pepper. Pour directly into the pan with the vegetables and move around to mix well. Scrape from the sides with a plastic or wooden spatula. Add the goat's cheese and herbs and season with salt and pepper.

Cover the pan with a lid and cook over medium heat for 5–8 minutes. The centre should still shake slightly but not be translucent. Remove the pan from the heat and set aside for 5 minutes.

Slice the frittata into portions and serve.

Tip:
Serve with a nice green salad or some grainy toast if you like.

ZUCCHINI NOODLE SALAD
WITH CORN & PINE NUTS

PREP: **8 MINUTES** // SERVES: **2** // Ⓥ

2 large zucchini
1 large carrot
1 large corncob, husk and silk removed
175 g (1 cup) halved cherry tomatoes
6 large basil leaves, torn
3 tablespoons finely grated parmesan
3 tablespoons pine nuts, toasted

DRESSING
80 ml (⅓ cup) olive oil
1 tablespoon dijon mustard
2 teaspoons maple syrup or honey
1 teaspoon freshly ground black pepper
1 teaspoon sea salt
2 tablespoons light mayonnaise
1 tablespoon Worcestershire sauce
1 tablespoon lemon juice

Start by making the zucchini noodles using a spiraliser. If you don't have a spiraliser, use a vegetable peeler to shave the zucchini lengthways, then cut the shavings into noodle-like strands. Place the zucchini noodles in a large bowl, then spiralise the carrot the same way and add to the bowl with the zucchini.

....

Shave the kernels off the corncob using a sharp knife. Add the corn to the bowl with the carrot and zucchini. Add the cherry tomatoes and the basil and toss to combine.

....

Mix all of the ingredients for the dressing in a bowl. If it is too thick, add a splash of water. Add the dressing to the shaved vegetables a little at a time until they are lightly coated.

....

Divide the salad between two bowls. Top with the parmesan and toasted pine nuts.

....

DONE!

Tip:
Try adding some protein to this salad in the form of chicken breast or firm-fleshed white fish.

ROASTED BRUSSELS SPROUT
& QUINOA SALAD

PREP: **8 MINUTES** // COOK: **12 MINUTES** // SERVES: **2** // Ⓥ

**250 ml (1 cup) vegetable stock
   or water**
100 g (½ cup) quinoa, rinsed
3 tablespoons olive oil
**200 g brussels sprouts,
   cut into quarters**
1 pomegranate
135 g (3 cups) rocket leaves
**3 tablespoons toasted and
   chopped pecans**
60 g (½ cup) crumbled goat's cheese
1 tablespoon maple syrup
zest and juice of 1 lemon
**sea salt and freshly ground
   black pepper**

Bring the vegetable stock or water to the boil in a saucepan. Add the quinoa and cook for 10 minutes over medium heat, or until the quinoa is tender with a slight bite. Set aside to cool slightly.

....

Meanwhile, heat 1 tablespoon of the olive oil in a frying pan over medium–high heat and sauté the brussels sprouts for 6–8 minutes, or until slightly toasted and soft.

....

Cut the pomegranate in half and hold it over a bowl with the cut side down; hit the skin side of the pomegranate with a wooden spoon to release the seeds. Repeat with the remaining half.

....

Combine the quinoa, brussels sprouts and pomegranate seeds in a bowl with 1 tablespoon of the olive oil, the rocket, pecans and half of the goat's cheese. Dress with the remaining olive oil, the maple syrup, lemon zest and juice and season to taste. Toss to coat and divide between two plates. Top with the remaining goat's cheese and some more freshly ground pepper.

MEXICAN QUINOA BOWL FOR YOU & A MATE

PREP: **10 MINUTES** // COOK: **10 MINUTES** // SERVES: **2** // Ⓥ

2 corn tortillas
250 ml (1 cup) vegetable stock
    or water
100 g (½ cup) quinoa, rinsed
3 tomatoes, diced
1 large corncob, husk and silk removed,
    kernels shaved off using a knife
2 jalapeño chillies, finely diced
1 white onion, finely diced
1 handful of coriander leaves,
    roughly chopped
1 lime
sea salt and freshly ground
    black pepper
2 teaspoons olive oil, plus extra
    for dressing
1 handful of watercress
100 g (½ cup) canned black beans,
    rinsed and drained
1 large avocado, peeled, halved
    and destoned
2 tablespoons Greek yoghurt
chia seeds, to serve

Preheat the oven to 190°C. Bake the corn tortillas on the oven rack for 5 minutes, or until crisp. Set aside.

Bring the vegetable stock or water to the boil in a saucepan over high heat. Add the quinoa, lower the heat and simmer, covered, for 10 minutes. Turn off the heat and leave it covered for another 10 minutes.

Meanwhile, place the tomato, shaved corn, jalapeño, onion, half of the coriander and the juice of ½ a lime in a mixing bowl. Season with salt and pepper to taste, add the olive oil and mix well.

Place the watercress in a bowl and add a little extra olive oil, salt and a squeeze of lime juice to taste.

Season the cooked quinoa lightly with salt and olive oil. Divide between two bowls. Season the black beans with salt and a squeeze of lime juice and divide between the bowls. Add the tomato mixture to each bowl and top with the avocado halves and yoghurt. Add the watercress and finish with a crispy corn tortilla, a sprinkling of chia seeds and the remaining coriander.

Tip:
This meal is also great with added protein, such as chicken or steak.

CREAMY CAULI & KALE SOUP

PREP: **8 MINUTES** // COOK: **20 MINUTES** // **MAKE AHEAD** // SERVES: **6** // ⓥ

1 tablespoon olive oil
1 onion, diced
1 large garlic clove, crushed
80 ml (⅓ cup) mild curry paste
50 g (¼ cup) jasmine rice
1.5 kg cauliflower (about 1½ heads),
    trimmed and roughly chopped
1 litre (4 cups) vegetable stock
250 ml (1 cup) coconut cream
40 g (1 cup) roughly chopped kale
    leaves, central stems removed
2 tablespoons roughly chopped
    flat-leaf parsley leaves
sea salt and freshly ground
    black pepper
wholegrain bread or naan,
    to serve (optional)

Heat the oil in a large saucepan over medium heat and add the onion and garlic. Cook for about 3 minutes, or until softened. Add the curry paste and cook, stirring, for about 1 minute, or until fragrant.

Add the rice, cauliflower, stock and 500 ml (2 cups) of cold water to the pan and bring to the boil. Reduce the heat to a simmer and stir occasionally for about 15 minutes, or until the rice and cauliflower are tender. Set aside for 5 minutes to cool.

Place half of the cauliflower mixture into a blender and blend until smooth and thick. Return the blended soup to the mixture in the pan and return the pan to the heat. Add the coconut cream and kale along with the parsley and season with salt and pepper to taste.

Divide the soup between bowls and serve hot, with some crusty wholegrain bread or naan (if using).

Tip: This is a great one to freeze in portions for speedy lunches or dinners.

ROASTED CHICKPEAS WITH CRUNCHY RADISH & CAULIFLOWER RICE

PREP: **8 MINUTES** // COOK: **12 MINUTES** // SERVES: **2** // Ⓥ

½ large cauliflower, cut into florets
2 tablespoons olive oil, plus extra
   for drizzling
160 g (1 cup) canned chickpeas,
   rinsed and drained
¼ teaspoon ground cumin
¼ teaspoon ground coriander
2 large radishes
½ cup marinated red capsicum,
   drained and sliced
90 g (2 cups) rocket leaves
juice of 1 large lemon
2 teaspoons maple syrup
sea salt and freshly ground
   black pepper

Steam the cauliflower for 4 minutes in the microwave or 6 minutes on the stovetop. Place the florets in a food processor and blitz using a pulsing action so as not to over-process. It should start to resemble small grains of rice. Alternatively, you can chop the florets with a large knife until you get the same crumb size.

Heat a frying pan over medium–high heat and add a drizzle of olive oil. Add the chickpeas, cumin and coriander. Move the chickpeas around so as not to burn them and toast for 4–6 minutes, or until they have a nice colour.

Finely slice the radishes using a mandoline over a bowl of iced water to remove some of the bitter flavour. Drain and dry them gently.

Combine the cauliflower rice, chickpeas and radish slices in a bowl and add the capsicum and rocket. Dress with the olive oil, lemon juice and maple syrup and season with salt and pepper.

Tip:
This salad goes really well with chicken or white fish if you need extra protein.

FRESH CUCUMBER & MILLET SALAD

PREP: **5 MINUTES** // COOK: **20 MINUTES** // SERVES: **2** // Ⓥ

40 g (½ cup) millet
250 ml (1 cup) water or
vegetable stock
2 continental cucumbers, peeled,
halved and seeds scooped out with
a spoon, then sliced
½ cup marinated red capsicum,
drained and sliced
3 tablespoons sunflower seeds, toasted
1 large avocado, diced
40 g (½ cup) shredded red cabbage
45 g (1 cup) rocket leaves
lime juice, to serve
olive oil, to serve

DRESSING
3 tablespoons apple cider vinegar
2 tablespoons maple syrup
1 tablespoon lime juice
1 tablespoon extra-virgin olive oil

Start by toasting the millet in a dry frying pan over medium heat until lightly toasted and aromatic. Bring the water or stock to the boil in a saucepan. Add the toasted millet, lower the heat to a simmer and cook for 15 minutes. Remove from the heat and stand for 5 minutes.

Meanwhile, mix the dressing ingredients together in a small bowl.

In a large bowl, combine the cucumber, capsicum, sunflower seeds, avocado, cabbage and the dressing. Toss well.

Stir the cooked millet with a fork and then mix it through the salad. Top with the rocket leaves, squeeze some lime juice over and drizzle with the olive oil.

A PRAWN SALAD
WITH A PEANUT TWIST

PREP: **10 MINUTES** // COOK: **6 MINUTES** // SERVES: **2**

10 king prawns, peeled and deveined
sea salt and freshly ground
    black pepper
1 tablespoon grapeseed oil
1 large zucchini, peeled into ribbons
    with a vegetable peeler
1 large carrot, peeled into ribbons
    with a vegetable peeler
¼ wombok, shredded
8 Thai basil leaves
6 mint leaves
1 handful of coriander leaves and stalks,
    finely chopped
sesame seeds, toasted, to serve

DRESSING
1 tablespoon smooth peanut butter
1 tablespoon maple syrup or honey
1 tablespoon apple cider vinegar
juice of ½ lime
2 teaspoons toasted sesame oil

Heat a frying pan over medium–high heat. Season the prawns with salt and pepper. Add the grapeseed oil to the pan with the prawns and cook on each side for 2–3 minutes, or until opaque. Remove from the heat and set aside.

In a small bowl, combine the dressing ingredients and adjust the seasoning if required.

Combine the vegetables and herbs in a large bowl. Mix some of the dressing through the vegetable mixture.

Divide the vegetable mixture between two plates. Add the prawns, drizzle with the rest of the dressing and sprinkle over some sesame seeds to finish.

NAILED IT!

TUNA SALAD WITH CUCUMBER, CELERY & DILL

PREP: **8 MINUTES** // SERVES: **2**

2 x 185 g cans tuna in oil or water
2 continental cucumbers, peeled and
   finely sliced
1 large celery stalk, finely sliced
2 tablespoons finely chopped dill fronds
2 tablespoons light mayonnaise or
   olive oil mayonnaise
1 tablespoon lemon juice, plus extra
   for drizzling
2 teaspoons dijon mustard
1 tablespoon olive oil, plus extra
   for drizzling
2 teaspoons maple syrup or honey
2 tablespoons chopped chives
2 tablespoons finely chopped
   cornichons
8 basil leaves
½ red capsicum, deseeded and
   finely sliced
sea salt and freshly ground
   black pepper
10 red or yellow witlof leaves,
   washed and dried, to serve

Drain the tuna and flake with a fork into a large bowl. Add all the remaining ingredients except the witlof leaves to the bowl and mix well. Check the seasoning, making sure there is a balance of salt, savoury and acid.

....

Divide the salad between two bowls and drizzle with a little extra olive oil and lemon juice and season with salt. Serve with the witlof leaves as little bowls for the salad.

GRILLED CHICKEN SALAD
WITH TAHINI &
LEMON DRESSING

PREP: 6 MINUTES // COOK: 10 MINUTES // MAKE AHEAD (CHICKEN) // SERVES: 2

1 large chicken breast fillet
(about 240 g)
sea salt and freshly ground
black pepper
2 tablespoons olive oil, plus extra
for drizzling
lemon juice, for drizzling
50 g (2 cups) shredded silverbeet
leaves, central stems removed
10 cherry tomatoes, halved
70 g (½ cup) walnuts, toasted
60 g (½ cup) crumbled goat's cheese
8 mint leaves, torn

DRESSING
juice of 1 lemon
3 tablespoons tahini
2 teaspoons maple syrup or honey
¼ teaspoon ground coriander
sea salt and freshly ground
black pepper

Preheat the oven to 200°C.

Combine the dressing ingredients in a small bowl, making sure to adjust the taste with more salt, acid or sweetness to your liking. Set aside.

Heat an ovenproof frying pan over high heat. Slice the chicken breast horizontally to make two pieces of the same thickness. Season with salt and pepper to taste. Pour the olive oil into the hot pan and carefully add the two pieces of chicken. Cook for 1 minute on each side, then transfer to the oven for 4 minutes. Remove from the oven, transfer the chicken to a plate and drizzle with a little lemon juice and olive oil.

In the same pan, cook the silverbeet for 2–3 minutes, or until just wilted. Add the tomatoes and cook until heated through. Remove from the heat, add the walnuts and goat's cheese and toss together. Divide the mixture between two bowls, then shred the chicken into bite-sized pieces and add to each bowl.

Drizzle the dressing over each bowl, scatter over the mint leaves and serve.

SESAME CHICKEN & BROCCOLINI STIR-FRY

PREP: **8 MINUTES** // COOK: **10 MINUTES** // SERVES: **2**

2 large chicken breast fillets
    (about 240 g each), cut into strips
sea salt and freshly ground
    black pepper
2 tablespoons sesame oil
1 large carrot, finely sliced
    on the diagonal
1 onion, roughly chopped
1 garlic clove, grated
2 teaspoons freshly grated ginger
4 broccolini stems, chopped into
    bite-sized pieces
3 tablespoons soy sauce or tamari
    (gluten-free soy sauce)
1 tablespoon lime juice
40 g (½ cup) bean sprouts, rinsed
zest of 1 lime, to serve
1 tablespoon toasted sesame seeds,
    to serve
1 handful of coriander leaves, to serve

In a bowl, season the chicken pieces with salt and pepper. Heat a large frying pan or wok over high heat and let it get smoky. Add 1 tablespoon of the sesame oil. Carefully add the chicken and stir-fry, stirring constantly, for 4–5 minutes.

Add the carrot, onion, garlic, ginger and broccolini with the soy sauce or tamari and lime juice. Stir-fry for 3 minutes, or until the veggies are nice and golden but still with a bit of crunch. Season with salt and pepper to taste and add the bean sprouts and remaining sesame oil.

Divide the stir-fry between two plates and top with the lime zest, sesame seeds and coriander.

EASY!

Tip:
A smoking hot wok is essential for a flavourful stir-fry.

CHICKEN YAKITORI WITH SUGAR SNAPS, SHIITAKE & SESAME RICE

PREP: **10 MINUTES** // COOK: **15 MINUTES** // SERVES: **2**

6 bamboo skewers, soaked in water
    (or use metal ones)
200 g (1 cup) jasmine or basmati rice
3 boneless, skinless chicken thighs
    (about 110 g each), cut into
    bite-sized pieces
1 large chicken breast fillet (about
    240 g), cut into bite-sized pieces
125 ml (½ cup) soy sauce or tamari
    (gluten-free soy sauce)
3 tablespoons maple syrup or honey
zest of 1 lime
1 tablespoon lime juice
2 teaspoons freshly grated ginger
2 tablespoons toasted sesame oil,
    plus extra for drizzling
6 large shiitake mushrooms,
    stems trimmed
light olive oil, for cooking and drizzling
75 g (1 cup) sugar snap peas, sliced
    lengthways down the middle
sea salt
2 spring onions, finely sliced
1 tablespoon sesame seeds, toasted

Preheat the oven to 200°C.

Place the rice in a saucepan with 375 ml (1½ cups) of water and bring to the boil. Lower the heat to a simmer, cover and cook for 10 minutes. After 10 minutes, remove from the heat and leave the lid on for another 10 minutes.

Meanwhile, place the chicken in a bowl and add the soy sauce or tamari, maple syrup or honey, lime zest and juice, ginger and 1 tablespoon of the sesame oil. Mix well using your hands, then transfer to the fridge to marinate for 5 minutes. When ready, thread the chicken onto the skewers, reserving the marinade.

Heat a large frying pan over medium–high heat. Coat the mushrooms with the remaining sesame oil and fry, being careful not to burn them. Move them around constantly for about 5 minutes, or until soft and slightly caramelised. Remove from the pan and set aside.

Using the same frying pan, heat some olive oil on high heat and sauté the sugar snap peas for about 2 minutes to quickly char. Remove from the pan and set aside with the mushrooms.

Heat the same frying pan over medium–high heat. Add the chicken skewers and sear for about 1½ minutes on each side to get a nice char. Lay the skewers on a baking tray and transfer to the oven to cook for another 5 minutes. Remove and set aside to rest.

Divide the rice between two bowls, drizzle with a little extra sesame oil and olive oil, and season with salt. Divide the mushrooms between the bowls, followed by the sugar snap peas, and top each bowl with three chicken skewers. Top with sliced spring onion and toasted sesame seeds.

CLASSIC LAMB KEBABS
WITH CUCUMBER YOGHURT

PREP: 10 MINUTES // COOK: 15 MINUTES // SERVES: 2

6 bamboo skewers, soaked in water (or use metal ones)
500 g lamb mince
2 tablespoons olive oil
60 g (½ cup) finely chopped flat-leaf parsley leaves
1 garlic clove, finely grated
1 small onion, diced
1 tablespoon red wine vinegar
1 teaspoon ground cumin
1 teaspoon ground coriander
½ teaspoon smoked paprika
1 tablespoon sea salt
freshly ground black pepper
95 g (½ cup) couscous
125 ml (½ cup) boiling water
olive oil, for drizzling and cooking
lemon juice, for drizzling
1 handful of mixed flat-leaf parsley, dill and coriander leaves, dressed with lemon juice, olive oil and salt, to serve

CUCUMBER YOGHURT
125 g (½ cup) Greek yoghurt
1 small Lebanese cucumber, peeled and finely chopped
juice of ½ lemon
8 mint leaves, finely chopped
sea salt and freshly ground black pepper, to taste

Combine the lamb, olive oil, parsley, garlic, onion, vinegar, spices, salt and pepper in a bowl, using your hands to mix well. Squeeze the mixture tightly onto each skewer to form a sausage shape and set aside on baking paper until ready to cook.

Place the couscous in a wide, flat container and add the boiling water. Cover with plastic wrap and set aside for about 5 minutes to allow the couscous to absorb the liquid. Scrape with a fork to break up any lumps and drizzle with some olive oil and lemon juice to taste.

Place all of the cucumber yoghurt ingredients in a small bowl and mix well.

Heat a frying pan over medium–high heat and add a little olive oil. Cook the lamb skewers for about 2–3 minutes on each side, or until cooked through. Transfer to a plate to rest.

Spoon some couscous onto each plate and top with 2–3 tablespoons of the cucumber yoghurt. Lay two or three skewers on each. Top with the herb salad and serve.

BUN-LESS BEEF BURGER WITH MELTED ONIONS, AVO & GRILLED RADICCHIO

PREP: **10 MINUTES** // COOK: **16 MINUTES** // MAKE AHEAD (PATTIES) // SERVES: **2**

sea salt and freshly ground
    black pepper
300 g beef mince
1 avocado
juice of 1 lime
2 small onions, finely sliced
2 tablespoons olive oil
2 tablespoons balsamic vinegar
4 radicchio or witlof leaves,
    washed and dried
4 large cos lettuce leaves,
    washed and dried
red wine vinegar
45 g (½ cup) shaved parmesan
2 teaspoons dijon mustard

Mix some salt and pepper through the mince and form two large patties, about 2 cm thick. Set aside.

Scoop the avocado flesh into a bowl and mash with a fork. Add some lime juice to taste and set aside.

Heat a chargrill pan over low heat. In a bowl, coat the onion with half of the olive oil. Turn the heat up to high and add the onion to the pan, moving it constantly so it doesn't burn. Once the onion starts to caramelise (about 5 minutes) add the balsamic vinegar and stir quickly as the vinegar evaporates. Add a pinch of salt and set the onion aside in a bowl.

Clean the pan with paper towel and reduce the heat to low. Lightly coat the radicchio or witlof with the remaining olive oil. Toss it onto the chargrill pan for a quick char on both sides, then set aside.

Season the patties well with salt and pepper and lay them on the chargrill pan over medium–high heat. Cook on each side for 3 minutes and set aside, covered, for an extra 10 minutes.

While the patties are resting, mix the cos leaves with salt, pepper, a few drops of red wine vinegar and half the parmesan and divide between two plates, with the radicchio or witlof alongside. Place the patties beside the salad and top with the mashed avocado, onion, the remaining parmesan and more freshly ground pepper. Serve with some mustard on the side.

THE BEST BAKED VEGGIES WITH QUINOA

PREP: 9 MINUTES // **COOK: 13 MINUTES** // **SERVES: 2** // Ⓥ

100 g (½ cup) quinoa
1 cup cauliflower florets
1 sweet potato, peeled and cut into
   2 cm cubes
1 large baked onion, peeled and
   thickly sliced (see Note)
3 tablespoons olive oil
1 garlic clove, finely chopped
2 teaspoons dried oregano
1 teaspoon dried marjoram
2 teaspoons smoked paprika
2 cups roughly chopped silverbeet
   leaves, central stems removed
1 tablespoon red wine vinegar
sea salt
1 handful of flat-leaf parsley leaves,
   roughly chopped
3 tablespoons pine nuts, toasted

Preheat the oven to 190°C.

Place the quinoa in a saucepan with 250 ml (1 cup) of water and bring to the boil over high heat. Cover and lower the heat to a simmer. Cook for 10 minutes, then turn off the heat and set aside, covered, for a further 10 minutes.

Meanwhile, place all of the vegetables except the silverbeet in an ovenproof frying pan with 2 tablespoons of the olive oil, plus the garlic, dried herbs and spices. Sauté on high heat for 3 minutes, or until starting to colour, then transfer to the oven for 10 minutes, or until fork tender. Add the silverbeet at the very last minute to wilt slightly.

Remove the veggies from the oven, add the remaining olive oil and the vinegar and season with salt. Mix with the quinoa and divide between two plates, finishing with the parsley and pine nuts.

Note: To bake an onion, cut it in half, leaving the skin on. Sear in an oiled ovenproof frying pan with the cut-side down until blackened. Transfer to a preheated 200°C oven, skin-side down, and bake for 12 minutes. Cool completely.

BALSAMIC LENTIL
SALAD – *SORTED!*

PREP: **5 MINUTES** // SERVES: **2** // Ⓥ

1 x 400 g can lentils, drained and rinsed
½ red capsicum, deseeded and diced
½ green capsicum, deseeded and diced
½ yellow capsicum, deseeded and diced
1 continental cucumber, diced
90 g (2 cups) rocket leaves
¼ red onion, finely diced
3 tablespoons chopped flat-leaf
   parsley leaves

DRESSING
3 tablespoons balsamic vinegar
2 teaspoons olive oil
1 teaspoon dijon mustard
1 teaspoon maple syrup
½ garlic clove, finely chopped
sea salt and freshly ground
   black pepper

In a large bowl, combine the lentils, capsicum, cucumber, rocket, onion and parsley.

Place all of the dressing ingredients in a small bowl and whisk well.

Pour the dressing over the salad and toss to combine.

Enjoy the salad at room temperature or chilled.

Tip:
Pack the salad and dressing separately and you have a great on-the-go lunch. Boom!

ROASTED SWEET POTATO WITH CAULIFLOWER PUREE, ALMONDS & SPINACH

PREP: **8 MINUTES** // COOK: **20 MINUTES** // SERVES: **2** // (V)

2 small sweet potatoes, scrubbed
½ cauliflower, broken into florets
1 large garlic clove, peeled
sea salt and freshly ground
    black pepper
zest and juice of ½ lemon
2 tablespoons olive oil, plus extra
    for frying
1 tablespoon maple syrup or honey
80 g (2 cups) roughly chopped
    English spinach leaves
1 tablespoon sherry vinegar
6 basil leaves
80 g (½ cup) almonds, toasted
    and chopped

Preheat the oven to 200°C.

Poke some holes in the sweet potatoes with a fork and microwave for 7–10 minutes, turning over after 5 minutes, until tender. Place them in the oven to crisp up and keep warm while you prepare the rest of the dish.

Meanwhile, place the cauliflower and garlic in a saucepan and fill halfway with water. Cover and boil for 8–10 minutes, or until tender. Drain and transfer to a blender with some salt and pepper and a squeeze of lemon juice. Blend until very smooth, adding a little water if necessary. Check the seasoning and adjust if needed.

Remove the sweet potatoes from the oven and lightly press with a tea towel to flatten out to look like steaks. Heat 1 tablespoon of the olive oil in a frying pan over medium–high heat and sear the sweet potatoes for 4 minutes on each side to caramelise. Season with salt and pepper and drizzle with the maple syrup or honey.

Divide the cauliflower puree between two plates. Drizzle with the remaining olive oil and sprinkle the lemon zest over the puree. Place the sweet potato on top.

In a frying pan over high heat, heat some extra olive oil and toss in the spinach. Sauté quickly to wilt, then sprinkle with some salt and the sherry vinegar. Remove from the heat and divide it between the plates, on top of each sweet potato. Finish with the basil leaves and almonds.

SALTY & SWEET QUINOA & APPLE SALAD

PREP: **10 MINUTES** // CHILL: **10 MINUTES** // SERVES: **2** // Ⓥ

80 g (2 cups) loosely packed chopped kale leaves, central stems removed
1 large apple, cored and chopped (I like to use pink lady apples)
100 g (½ cup) tricolor quinoa, cooked in 250 ml (1 cup) of water, cooled completely
50 g (½ cup) walnuts, lightly toasted and roughly chopped
40 g (⅓ cup) dried cranberries
30 g (¼ cup) goat's cheese, crumbled

DRESSING
80 ml (⅓ cup) olive oil
3 tablespoons lemon juice
1 tablespoon honey or maple syrup
1 teaspoon dijon mustard
pinch of sea salt

Whisk together all of the dressing ingredients in a jar or small bowl.

Place the kale in a salad bowl, pour a quarter of the whisked dressing over it and toss until the kale is evenly coated. Cover the bowl and chill in the fridge for 7–10 minutes.

Remove the kale from the fridge and add the apple, quinoa, walnuts and cranberries to the bowl.

Pour the remaining dressing over the salad, then toss. Top with the goat's cheese and serve.

DONE!

BAJA FISH TACOS
WITH **TANGY SLAW**

PREP: 10 MINUTES // COOK: 10 MINUTES // SERVES: 2

3 x 110–140 g skinless mahi-mahi fillets
   (or other firm-fleshed white fish)
2–3 chipotle chillies in adobo sauce,
   finely chopped, plus 2 tablespoons
   adobo sauce
1 garlic clove, crushed
2 tablespoons melted butter
1 teaspoon finely chopped oregano leaves
olive oil, for cooking
4 flour tortillas
juice of 1 lime
salsa, to serve (optional)

SLAW

100 g (1½ cups) shredded green
   or red cabbage
½ red onion, finely sliced
3 radishes, finely sliced with
   a mandoline or sharp knife
1 handful of coriander leaves, chopped
2 spring onions, chopped
juice of ½ lime
1–2 tablespoons maple syrup
   or honey (optional)
sea salt and freshly ground
   black pepper

CREMA (OPTIONAL)

125 g (⅓ cup) light sour cream
juice of ½ lime
2 teaspoons maple syrup or honey
1–2 tablespoons finely chopped
   coriander leaves

To make the slaw, combine the cabbage, onion, radish, coriander and spring onion in a bowl with the lime juice and maple syrup or honey (if using). Season with salt and pepper to taste. Refrigerate until ready to eat.

If making the crema, combine the ingredients in a small bowl and refrigerate until ready to eat.

Preheat the oven to 180°C.

Prepare the fish fillets by seasoning lightly with salt and pepper on both sides. Combine the chipotle, adobo sauce, garlic, melted butter and oregano in a small dish and baste the fish on both sides using all (or most) of the sauce.

Heat a little olive oil in an ovenproof frying pan over medium–high heat. Sear both sides of the fish fillets for 1½–2 minutes, or until nicely browned and easy to flip over. Transfer the pan to the oven and bake for 4–6 minutes, or until the fish flakes easily – this will depend on the thickness of the fish and how well done you like it.

Remove the pan from the oven and set aside to rest for about 3 minutes. While the fish is resting, warm the tortillas in the oven. Flake the fish into small chunks and squeeze a little lime juice over it.

To assemble the tacos, place the fish and slaw in the warm tortillas and serve with the crema and salsa on the side (if using).

SPICY MOROCCAN CHICKEN BOWL

PREP: **5 MINUTES** // COOK: **20 MINUTES** // **MAKE AHEAD (CHICKEN)** // SERVES: **2**

1–2 teaspoons smoked paprika
2 teaspoons ground cumin
¼ teaspoon ground cinnamon
¼ teaspoon cayenne pepper
½ teaspoon sea salt
½ teaspoon freshly ground black pepper
½ teaspoon ground coriander
2 tablespoons olive oil
450 g chicken breast fillets, sliced into thin strips
1 small onion, finely sliced
2 garlic cloves, finely chopped
2 red capsicums, deseeded and chopped
3 carrots, chopped
3 tablespoons tomato paste
1 small chipotle chilli in adobo sauce, finely chopped
500 ml (2 cups) chicken stock
400 g (2 cups) cooked chickpeas, rinsed and drained
zest and juice of 1 lime
3 tablespoons coriander leaves, plus extra to serve
2 cups cooked couscous
40 g (⅓ cup) chopped pistachios
goat's cheese, crumbled

In a small bowl, mix the smoked paprika, cumin, cinnamon, cayenne pepper, salt, pepper and ground coriander.

In a large frying pan over medium–high heat, heat 1 tablespoon of the olive oil to coat the bottom of the frying pan. Add the chicken and half of the spice mixture. Brown the chicken strips for about 6 minutes, or until cooked through. Remove the chicken from the frying pan and set aside.

Add the remaining olive oil to the same pan. Add the onion, garlic, capsicum and carrot and sauté for 4–5 minutes. Add the remaining spice mixture and sauté for another 15 seconds, stirring constantly. Return the chicken to the pan. Stir in the tomato paste, chipotle chilli, chicken stock and chickpeas. Bring to the boil, then reduce the heat and simmer for 5 minutes, or until the mixture thickens. Remove from the heat. Stir in the lime zest and juice and the coriander leaves.

Divide the couscous between serving bowls and top with the chopped pistachios and the chicken and chickpea mixture. Scatter on the crumbled goat's cheese and the extra coriander.

GINGER CHICKEN STIR-FRY
WITH SPRING VEGGIES

PREP: **5 MINUTES** // COOK: **15 MINUTES** // SERVES: **2**

2 tablespoons sesame oil
225 g chicken breast fillets, cut into
   2.5 cm pieces
125 ml (½ cup) chicken stock
1–2 tablespoons soy sauce or tamari
   (gluten-free soy sauce)
1 garlic clove, crushed
2 teaspoons freshly grated ginger
½ red onion, sliced
1 bunch of Dutch carrots, trimmed
   and halved lengthways
2 celery stalks, sliced on the diagonal
½ red capsicum, deseeded and sliced
75 g (1 cup) sugar snap peas, sliced
   lengthways down the middle
280 g (1½ cups) steamed rice
toasted sesame seeds (optional)

Heat the sesame oil in a large frying pan or wok over medium–high heat. Add the chicken and sauté for 4–5 minutes, or until brown. Add the stock, soy sauce or tamari, garlic and ginger. Cover, reduce the heat to medium and cook for 5 minutes, stirring occasionally.

....

Add all of the vegetables to the pan. Cover and cook for a further 5 minutes, stirring occasionally, until the chicken is no longer pink in the centre and the veggies are tender crisp.

....

Divide the rice between two plates, spoon the stir-fry on top and sprinkle with the toasted sesame seeds (if using).

....

EASY!

CUBAN BLACK BEAN BOWL

PREP: 7 MINUTES // COOK: **20 MINUTES** // MAKE AHEAD (BEANS) // SERVES: **2**

3 tablespoons olive oil
4 garlic cloves, crushed with the flat
    side of a knife
1 tablespoon finely grated orange zest
3 tablespoons orange juice
3 tablespoons lime juice
2 tablespoons lemon juice
2 teaspoons ground cumin
2 tablespoons chopped coriander
    leaves, plus extra to serve
½ teaspoon cayenne pepper
2 teaspoons dried oregano
¾ teaspoon sea salt
½ teaspoon freshly ground
    black pepper
450 g chicken breast fillets, cut into
    4 cm pieces
3 cups cooked quinoa
lime wedges, to serve

SPICED BLACK BEANS
1 x 425 g can black beans, drained
    and rinsed
250 ml (1 cup) warm water
1 teaspoon sea salt
1 teaspoon ground cumin
½ teaspoon chipotle chilli powder
2–3 tablespoons chopped
    coriander leaves
80 ml (⅓ cup) lime juice

SALSA
2 large mangoes, cut into 2.5 cm cubes
1 habañero chilli, finely chopped
½ small red onion, finely chopped
2 tablespoons lime juice
2 tablespoons chopped
    coriander leaves

Combine 2 tablespoons of the olive oil in a bowl with the garlic, orange zest, orange juice, lime juice, lemon juice, cumin, coriander, cayenne pepper and oregano. Add the salt and pepper and stir. Add the chicken, mix well and set aside to marinate for at least 10 minutes.

To make the spiced black beans, place the black beans, warm water, salt, cumin and chilli powder in a saucepan and bring to the boil. Reduce the heat and simmer for 7–10 minutes. Remove from the heat, strain and gently mix through the fresh coriander and lime juice. Reserve 1 cup of the beans for the dish – store leftovers in the fridge for up to 3 days (or freeze for longer).

Meanwhile, prepare the salsa. Combine all of the ingredients in a medium bowl and mix well. Refrigerate until ready to serve.

Heat a frying pan over medium–high heat. Add the remaining tablespoon of olive oil. Drain the chicken from the marinade and add just one layer of chicken to the pan to cook for 3–5 minutes, or until the chicken is caramelised on the outside and cooked all the way through. Remove to a plate. Add additional oil if needed and repeat with the remaining chicken.

Divide the quinoa between two bowls. Top with some of the mango salsa, the black beans and chicken. Top with the extra coriander leaves and serve with lime wedges on the side.

Tip:
Store leftover mango salsa in the fridge for up to 3 days. It's great for snacks and salads.

LEGENDARY LAMB
YIROS – *SO GOOD!*

PREP: 5 MINUTES // COOK: 15 MINUTES // MAKE AHEAD // SERVES: 2

225 g lamb mince
1½ tablespoons dried breadcrumbs
1 egg
2 tablespoons chopped flat-leaf
   parsley leaves
2 garlic cloves, finely chopped
½ teaspoon ground cumin
½ teaspoon sea salt
¼ teaspoon freshly ground
   black pepper
2 pita breads

TZATZIKI
250 g (1 cup) Greek yoghurt
1 Lebanese cucumber, grated
1 garlic clove, finely chopped
1 teaspoon extra-virgin olive oil
1 tablespoon chopped dill fronds
½ teaspoon sea salt
¼ teaspoon freshly ground
   black pepper
1 tablespoon lemon juice

TOMATO & CUCUMBER SALAD
1 large Lebanese cucumber, chopped
3 tomatoes, chopped
1 small red onion, finely diced
1 tablespoon chopped flat-leaf
   parsley leaves

Preheat the oven to 220°C. Line a baking tray with baking paper.

Combine all of the tzatziki ingredients in a bowl. Cover and refrigerate until ready to serve.

In a large mixing bowl, combine the lamb, breadcrumbs, egg, parsley, garlic, cumin, salt and pepper. Use your hands to mix well and then form the mixture into golf ball–sized meatballs. Place the meatballs on the prepared tray and bake for about 10 minutes, or until cooked through and no longer pink inside. Cooking time will vary, depending on the size of your meatballs.

While the meatballs are cooking, combine the salad ingredients in a serving dish. Season with salt and pepper to taste. When the meatballs are cooked through, remove them from the oven to rest.

Switch the oven to grill and lay the pita breads on a baking tray. Grill until lightly toasted on both sides. Remember to watch closely so they don't burn. When ready, cut open each pita bread.

To assemble the yiros, place two or three meatballs in each pita bread. Top with large spoonfuls of the tomato and cucumber salad. Serve with the tzatziki in small bowls and enjoy!

SIZZLING STEAK
FA-PITAS

PREP: **5 MINUTES** // COOK: **15 MINUTES** // SERVES: **2**

1 teaspoon ground cumin
1 teaspoon chipotle chilli powder
1 teaspoon sea salt
zest and juice of 1 lime, plus extra
    1 tablespoon lime juice
1 tablespoon Worcestershire sauce
3 large garlic cloves, crushed or
    finely chopped
225 g skirt steak
2 tablespoons olive oil, plus extra
    if needed
1 large red or brown onion, halved
    and sliced
2 red capsicums, deseeded and cut into
    5 mm thick slices
1 green capsicum, deseeded and cut
    into 5 mm thick slices
1 jalapeño chilli, finely chopped
2 large pita breads
3 tablespoons roughly chopped
    coriander leaves
1 baby cos lettuce, cut crossways
    into 2.5 cm wide pieces
crumbled feta, to serve

In a small bowl, whisk together the cumin, chipotle, salt, lime zest and juice, Worcestershire sauce and garlic to make a sauce.

Heat a large frying pan over medium–high heat. Pat the meat dry with paper towel. Add the olive oil to the hot pan, then add the steak. Pour over the sauce and cook the steak for 3–4 minutes on each side for medium–rare. Be sure to not let the sauce burn. Remove the steak to a chopping board, cover with foil and set aside to rest for 10 minutes. Cut across the grain into 1.5 cm wide strips.

In the same pan, add the onion to the remaining sauce and cook, stirring, for 4–5 minutes, or until softened. Stir in the capsicums and jalapeño. Cook, stirring, for 3 minutes, or until the capsicum begins to soften. Add more oil if needed.

Wrap the pita breads in foil and warm in a low oven, or leave them unwrapped and use a microwave.

Lay a pita bread on each plate and divide the steak between them, tipping any juices from the chopping board over the meat. Top with the coriander leaves and cos lettuce and scatter with the crumbled feta. Drizzle the extra lime juice over and serve.

DINNER?
DONE

CORE MEALS //

POST-WORKOUT MEALS //

ASPARAGUS RIBBON SALAD

PREP: **5 MINUTES** // MARINATE: **15 MINUTES** // SERVES: **2** //

150 g asparagus (about 8 stems), woody ends trimmed
90–135 g (2–3 cups) rocket leaves
3 tablespoons hazelnuts or walnuts, toasted and roughly chopped
crumbled goat's cheese, to serve

DRESSING
3 tablespoons olive oil
2 tablespoons lemon juice
2 teaspoons honey or maple syrup
1 small red onion, finely chopped
sea salt and freshly ground black pepper, to taste

Using a vegetable peeler, start from the tip of the asparagus stem and gently shave downwards to create thin ribbons. Once you only have the tip left, use a small paring knife to slice it down the middle. Place the ribbons and tips in a large bowl and set aside.

....

Place the dressing ingredients in a small bowl and whisk to combine. Toss the asparagus with the dressing until well coated. Set aside to marinate for 10–15 minutes.

....

Add the rocket to the asparagus and toss well, then top with the nuts and cheese.

....

EASY!

BEAN & BARLEY
SALAD – *SORTED!*

PREP: **10 MINUTES** // **MAKE AHEAD** // SERVES: **2** // Ⓥ

100 g (½ cup) canned chickpeas,
rinsed and drained
100 g (½ cup) canned cannellini beans,
rinsed and drained
100 g (½ cup) canned kidney beans,
rinsed and drained
½ continental cucumber, finely diced
1 tomato, finely diced
1 spring onion, finely chopped
½ red capsicum, deseeded and
finely diced
1 tablespoon each finely chopped dill,
mint and basil leaves
3 ½ cups cooked barley (see Note)
3 tablespoons olive oil
2 tablespoons red wine vinegar
1 tablespoon maple syrup or honey
sea salt and freshly ground
black pepper

In a large bowl, combine the chickpeas, cannellini and kidney beans with the cucumber, tomato, spring onion, capsicum, herbs and barley. Add the olive oil, vinegar and maple syrup or honey. Season with salt and pepper to taste. Divide between two bowls and serve.

Note: To cook the barley, bring 500 ml (2 cups) of water and 220 g (1 cup) of barley to the boil and cook for 20–30 minutes, until tender. Drain and set aside to cool. Barley will always have a bit of texture no matter how long you cook it for. This is due to the fibre and proteins the grain naturally contains.

THAI-STYLE QUINOA SALAD

PREP: **10 MINUTES** // SERVES: **2**

740 g (4 cups) cooked quinoa, chilled
1 large yellow capsicum, deseeded
    and sliced
1 large carrot, grated
1 continental cucumber, deseeded
    and sliced into batons
2 spring onions, finely sliced
3 tablespoons chopped coriander leaves
2 tablespoons each chopped basil
    and mint leaves
sea salt and freshly ground
    black pepper
1 small red chilli, deseeded and sliced

DRESSING
3 tablespoons lime juice
2 teaspoons fish sauce
1 tablespoon olive oil
2 tablespoons maple syrup or honey
¼ teaspoon chilli flakes

Make the dressing by whisking all of the ingredients together in a bowl until well combined.

....

Place the quinoa in a large serving bowl and add the capsicum, carrot, cucumber, spring onion, coriander, basil and mint. Add the dressing, toss well, season with salt and pepper and taste and adjust the seasoning if necessary. Serve topped with the sliced chilli.

....

DONE!

CAPSICUM SALAD

WITH WHITE BEANS

& FARRO

PREP: 10 MINUTES // **SERVES: 2** // Ⓥ

2 cups cooked farro (see Note)
olive oil, for drizzling
sea salt and freshly ground
   black pepper
1 cup marinated red capsicum,
   drained and sliced
200 g (1 cup) canned cannellini beans,
   rinsed and drained
3 tablespoons chopped capers
1 large garlic clove, grated
2 teaspoons grated lemon zest
1 tablespoon maple syrup or honey
½ teaspoon ground coriander
1 teaspoon smoked paprika
90 g (2 cups) rocket leaves
½ cup mixed fresh herbs (such as
   chives, parsley, snow pea sprouts
   and dill fronds)
50 g (⅓ cup) chopped toasted almonds
1 tablespoon sherry vinegar

Drizzle the cooked farro with a little olive oil and season with salt and pepper to taste.

Combine the capsicum, cannellini beans, capers, garlic, lemon zest, maple syrup or honey, ground coriander and paprika in a bowl and mix well. Add the farro, mix well and season with salt to taste.

Divide the mixture between two serving bowls or jars and add the rocket leaves, herbs and almonds. Dress with a little vinegar and olive oil.

Note: To cook the farro, place 120 g (½ cup) farro in a saucepan with 250 ml (1 cup) of water and bring to the boil. Simmer on medium–low heat for 20 minutes, or until tender. Remember that farro will still have a slight bite, no matter how long you cook it for.

Tip:
Use barley instead
of farro if you prefer.
See page 169
for cooking
instructions.

SPICY WALNUT TACOS

PREP: **13 MINUTES** // CHILL: **7 MINUTES** // SERVES: **2** // (V)

juice of ½ lime
1 tablespoon olive oil
sea salt and freshly ground
 black pepper
150 g (1 cup) cherry tomatoes,
 chopped
½ red capsicum, deseeded
 and chopped
½ green capsicum, deseeded
 and chopped
½ small red onion, chopped
½ cup chopped coriander leaves
corn taco shells, cabbage leaves or
 butter lettuce leaves, to be used
 as wraps

WALNUT TACO MIXTURE
100 g (1 cup) walnuts
1 tablespoon soy sauce or tamari
 (gluten-free soy sauce)
¼ teaspoon chipotle chilli powder
¼ teaspoon smoked paprika
1½ teaspoons extra-virgin olive oil

To make the walnut taco mixture, place all of the ingredients in a food processor and pulse just to mix: it should resemble beef mince.

....

Whisk the lime juice, olive oil, salt and pepper together in a bowl to make a dressing.

....

Place the chopped veggies in the bowl with the dressing. Fold in the coriander and chill in the fridge for 5–7 minutes.

....

Spoon the walnut taco mixture and the veggie mixture into your choice of shell or wrap to serve.

....

SO GOOD!

WARMING LEEK
& APPLE SOUP – *MMM!*

PREP: **5 MINUTES** // COOK: **20 MINUTES** // **MAKE AHEAD** // SERVES: **4** // Ⓥ

3 tablespoons olive oil
3 leeks, white and light green parts,
 washed and chopped
3 thyme sprigs, leaves picked and
 finely chopped
1 fennel bulb, cored and chopped
1 apple, peeled, cored and chopped
 (I like to use pink lady)
1 teaspoon ground turmeric
70 g (½ cup) walnut halves or
 hazelnuts, chopped and toasted,
 plus extra to serve
sea salt and freshly ground
 black pepper
1 litre (4 cups) vegetable stock
1 tablespoon maple syrup, to serve

Heat the olive oil in a large saucepan or stockpot over medium heat. Add the leek and thyme. Stir and sauté for 5 minutes, or until softened. Stir in the fennel and apple.

....

Add the turmeric to the pan and stir to coat all of the vegetables. Sauté for another 4 minutes, or until the fennel is softened. Stir in the nuts and season with salt and pepper. Add the vegetable stock and stir.

....

Bring the soup to the boil and simmer for 10 minutes, or until the vegetables and apple are very soft. Remove the soup from the heat. Carefully blend the mixture in batches until totally smooth.

....

Bring the pureed soup back to a simmer and serve hot with a drizzle of maple syrup and a sprinkle of extra nuts.

MISO VEGGIE SOUP

PREP: **5 MINUTES** // COOK: **10 MINUTES** // SERVES: **2** // Ⓥ

1 litre (4 cups) vegetable or
   chicken stock
2 cups sliced assorted mushrooms,
   or left whole if very small
2 carrots, finely sliced into rounds
2–3 spring onions, finely sliced
2–3 tablespoons white miso paste

Heat the stock with 500 ml (2 cups) of water in a large saucepan over medium heat. Bring to a simmer, then add the mushrooms and carrot. Simmer for 8–10 minutes, or until the carrot is tender. When ready to serve, add the spring onion and remove from the heat.

In a small bowl, whisk the miso with 3 tablespoons of the hot soup to form a paste. Stir back into the soup and serve.

Tip:
This soup would also be great with chicken or fish. Add it to the soup or serve it on the side.

BABY BOK CHOY
WITH QUINOA
& SHIITAKE

PREP: 8 MINUTES // **COOK: 20 MINUTES** // **SERVES: 2** // (V)

100 g (½ cup) quinoa, rinsed
1 tablespoon toasted sesame oil,
    plus extra for seasoning
4 baby bok choy, halved lengthways
2 leeks, white part only, washed
    and roughly chopped
8–10 shiitake mushrooms,
    finely sliced
1 garlic clove, grated
2 teaspoons freshly grated ginger
3 tablespoons soy sauce or tamari
    (gluten-free soy sauce)
1 tablespoon maple syrup or honey
sea salt and freshly ground
    black pepper
1 kaffir lime leaf, very finely sliced

Place the quinoa in a small saucepan with 250 ml (1 cup) of water and bring to the boil over high heat. Cover and lower the heat to a simmer. Cook for 10 minutes, then turn off the heat and set aside, covered, for a further 10 minutes.

Meanwhile, place a frying pan over high heat and add the sesame oil and bok choy. Cook for 4–6 minutes, or until the greens get a nice golden char on the cut sides. Add a little water to help steam them a bit, then remove to a plate and set aside.

In the same pan, lower the heat to medium and fry the leek, mushroom, garlic and ginger. Cook for 5 minutes, then add the soy sauce or tamari, maple syrup or honey and the bok choy and cook for another 5 minutes.

Season the cooked quinoa with some sesame oil and salt and pepper to taste. Divide the quinoa between two bowls and top with the mushroom and bok choy mixture, along with the pan juices. Scatter the sliced kaffir lime leaf over both plates and serve.

JOB DONE!

WHITE FISH
WITH HERBY LENTIL SALAD

PREP: **5 MINUTES** // COOK: **15 MINUTES** // SERVES: **2**

110 g (½ cup) brown lentils, rinsed
250 ml (1 cup) vegetable stock
125 ml (½ cup) dry white wine
1 dried bay leaf
1 thyme sprig
¼ teaspoon sea salt
1 tablespoon lemon juice
1 teaspoon maple syrup or honey
2 small garlic cloves, finely chopped
3 tablespoons extra-virgin olive oil
3 tablespoons chopped flat-leaf
    parsley leaves
1 tablespoon finely chopped basil
    leaves, plus extra leaves to serve
freshly ground black pepper
2 x 150 g gurnard or snapper fillets
2 tablespoons grapeseed oil
1 tablespoon finely grated lemon zest
1 large carrot, cut into matchsticks
1 large capsicum, deseeded and diced
½ small French shallot, finely diced
4 small radishes, finely sliced
1 tablespoon finely grated lemon zest

In a saucepan, combine the lentils, vegetable stock, white wine, bay leaf, thyme and salt. Bring to the boil, then reduce to medium–low heat and simmer for about 15 minutes, or until the lentils are tender.

Meanwhile, in a small bowl, whisk together the lemon juice, maple syrup or honey and garlic. Whisk in the olive oil until the dressing thickens. Whisk in the parsley and basil and season to taste with salt and pepper.

Season both sides of the fish with salt and pepper. Heat the grapeseed oil in a large frying pan over medium–high heat and cook the fish on one side for 3 minutes, or until golden brown. Flip the fish and cook for about 2 minutes on the other side.

Drain the lentils and remove the bay leaf and thyme. Combine the cooked lentils, carrot, capsicum, shallot and radish in a large bowl and season with salt and pepper. Pour some of the dressing over the lentil salad and toss to coat. Add more dressing if needed until the lentils are well coated. Divide between two plates and top with the fish, brushed with the remaining dressing and sprinkled with some lemon zest.

HONEY–SOY SALMON WITH MUSHROOMS & GREENS – *THE BEST!*

PREP: **5 MINUTES** // COOK: **15 MINUTES** // SERVES: **2**

225 g thick-cut salmon fillet, skin on, cut into two equal portions
3 bok choy, halved lengthways
115 g shiitake mushrooms, stems trimmed
3 tablespoons soy sauce or tamari (gluten-free soy sauce)
1 tablespoon sesame oil
1 teaspoon maple syrup or honey
1 teaspoon freshly grated ginger
sea salt and freshly ground black pepper
zest of ½ small orange
1 spring onion, chopped on the diagonal
sesame seeds, toasted, to serve
chilli flakes or sriracha chilli sauce, to serve

Preheat the oven to 180°C. Line two baking trays with baking paper.

Lay the salmon, skin-side down, on one tray, and the bok choy and mushrooms on the other.

Mix the soy sauce or tamari, sesame oil, maple syrup or honey and ginger together in a small bowl. Pour half over the salmon and half over the bok choy and mushrooms.

Season the salmon with salt and pepper and sprinkle the orange zest over it.

Bake both trays for about 10 minutes. When the bok choy is bright green and the mushrooms are tender, remove the tray from the oven. Continue cooking the salmon until opaque. The cooking time will vary depending on the thickness of the fillet.

Place the salmon fillets on top of the veggies and serve them in the tray. Top with the spring onion, toasted sesame seeds and chilli flakes or sriracha.

ENJOY!

SEARED SALMON
WITH NUTTY ZUCCHINI SALAD

PREP: **8 MINUTES** // COOK: **12 MINUTES** // SERVES: **2**

2 tablespoons olive oil,
   plus extra to serve
2 x 150 g salmon fillets, skin on
1 zucchini
1 carrot
1 small handful of dill fronds,
   very finely chopped
1 small handful of mint leaves,
   finely chopped, plus extra
   leaves to serve
80 g (½ cup) almonds, toasted
3 tablespoons pine nuts, toasted
3 tablespoons sunflower seeds
1 tablespoon maple syrup or honey
1 tablespoon apple cider vinegar
sea salt and freshly ground
   black pepper
zest and juice of 1 lemon, to serve

Heat a frying pan over medium–high heat. Add 1 tablespoon of the olive oil to coat the pan, then add the salmon, skin-side down. Cook for 5 minutes, then lower the heat to medium and turn the salmon over. Cook for a further 4–6 minutes, or until the salmon is cooked to your liking (see Note). Remove from the heat and set aside to rest.

Meanwhile, use a mandoline or vegetable peeler to finely slice the zucchini and carrot into ribbons, then use a sharp knife to cut the ribbons into noodle-like strands. Mix the zucchini, carrot, dill, mint, nuts and seeds in a bowl with the remaining olive oil, the maple syrup or honey and vinegar. Season with salt and pepper and adjust the seasoning if necessary: you want a nice balance of sweet, savoury, salty and citrusy.

Divide the vegetable mixture between two serving plates and place a piece of salmon on top of each. Sprinkle on the lemon zest and drizzle over the lemon juice and extra olive oil. Scatter on the mint leaves and serve.

Note: I usually like my salmon a bit rare in the centre, but you can cook it longer if you prefer.

CORE MEAL

CORIANDER & LIME CHICKEN
WITH AVO SAUCE

PREP: **8 MINUTES** // COOK: **15 MINUTES** // SERVES: **2**

**2 large chicken breast fillets
   (about 240 g each)**
**sea salt and freshly ground
   black pepper**
zest and juice of 2 limes
2 tablespoons vegetable oil
1 large avocado
1 garlic clove, peeled
1 handful of coriander leaves
**1 teaspoon soy sauce or tamari
   (gluten-free soy sauce) (optional)**
**2 baby cos lettuces or 1 large,
   halved lengthways and
   outer leaves removed**
1 tablespoon olive oil
1 corncob, husk and silk removed
3 tablespoons finely grated parmesan

Preheat the oven to 200°C.

Season the chicken with the salt, pepper and lime zest. Heat a frying pan over high heat, add the vegetable oil, then gently add the chicken breasts. Cook on each side for 1 minute to sear. Lower the heat to medium–low and cook for a further 3–5 minutes on each side, or until the chicken is cooked through. Remove from the heat and set aside to rest.

Meanwhile, scoop the avocado flesh into a blender along with the garlic clove, the juice of 1 lime, the coriander, soy sauce or tamari (if using), two pinches of sea salt and 125 ml (½ cup) of water. Blend until smooth. Spoon into small serving bowls.

Heat a chargrill pan over high heat or use a barbecue set on high. Coat the cos lettuce with a little olive oil and place on the hot grill, cut-side down. Sear for 2 minutes to get a nice char. Coat the corncob with the remaining olive oil. Grill for about 6 minutes, rolling it around so all of the kernels are cooked. Cut the corncob in half.

To serve, divide the grilled cos lettuce between two plates. Thickly slice the chicken, place on top of the cos and sprinkle with some parmesan. Place half a corncob on each plate and drizzle with the remaining lime juice. Serve with the avocado sauce on the side.

PESTO SPAGHETTI SQUASH
WITH PAN-FRIED CHICKEN

PREP: **5 MINUTES** // COOK: **20 MINUTES** // SERVES: **2**

**1 small–medium spaghetti squash
    (about 1.5 kg)**
1 tablespoon coconut oil
**2 large chicken breast fillets
    (about 240 g each)**
**sea salt and freshly ground
    black pepper**
½ teaspoon onion powder
**½ cup pesto (store-bought or
    see page 234 for a recipe)**

Preheat the oven to 220°C and line a large baking tray with foil or baking paper.

Cut the spaghetti squash in half lengthways using a large, sharp knife. Scoop out the seeds, then lay the squash halves face down on the prepared baking tray. Roast for about 20 minutes, or until the squash can be pierced easily with a fork. Set aside to cool.

When the squash is cool enough to handle, use a fork to scrape lengthways down the squash to release the spaghetti strings. Place the strings in a large bowl, then squeeze the squash strings between paper towel to remove any excess liquid.

Meanwhile, heat a large frying pan over medium–high heat and add the coconut oil. Season the chicken lightly with salt, pepper and onion powder, then fry for 5 minutes on each side, or until no longer pink in the centre. Remove from the pan and set aside to cool. Once cool enough to handle, cut the chicken into thick slices.

Place the chicken in the bowl with the spaghetti squash and add the pesto. Toss to combine and serve.

EASY!

HERBED CHICKEN WITH CRUNCHY BRUSSELS SPROUT & APPLE SALAD

PREP: **10 MINUTES** // COOK: **10 MINUTES** // SERVES: **2**

2 chicken breast fillets (about 150 g each), pounded with a meat mallet or rolling pin to flatten
1 handful of coriander leaves and stems, very finely chopped
3 tablespoons olive oil
zest and juice of 1 lemon, plus extra zest to serve
12 brussels sprouts, shaved with a mandoline or very sharp knife and soaked in cold water
1 apple, peeled, cored and cut into matchsticks
80 g (½ cup) walnuts, toasted and chopped
2 tablespoons maple syrup or honey
sea salt and freshly ground black pepper
1 avocado, peeled, destoned and quartered
6 basil leaves, finely sliced

Place the chicken breasts in a bowl and add the coriander along with 1 tablespoon of the olive oil and the lemon zest. Marinate for 3 minutes.

Heat a frying pan over medium–high heat with 1 tablespoon of the olive oil. Add the chicken breasts and cook for about 2–3 minutes on each side, or until the chicken is cooked through.

Drain the brussels sprouts and pat dry with paper towel. Place them in a bowl along with the apple, walnuts, maple syrup or honey and the remaining olive oil. Squeeze over some lemon juice, season with salt and pepper to taste and mix well.

Heat another frying pan over high heat. Add the avocado quarters with one cut-side down and cook for 2–3 minutes to get a nice char. Repeat with the other cut side. Remove from the heat and season with some lemon juice, salt and pepper.

Divide the chicken between serving plates. Squeeze over a little lemon juice and season with salt to taste. Place a nice mountain of the brussels sprouts mixture beside the chicken on each plate. Scatter the sliced basil over the top and finish with the warm avocado sprinkled with some extra lemon zest.

TURKEY MEATBALLS
IN TOMATO SAUCE

PREP: 10 MINUTES // COOK: 17 MINUTES // MAKE AHEAD // SERVES: 2

225 g extra-lean turkey mince
   (or use chicken mince if you prefer)
½ onion, grated
3 garlic cloves, finely chopped
⅓ cup flat-leaf parsley leaves,
   finely chopped
1 large egg
1 teaspoon dried oregano
½ teaspoon sea salt
½ teaspoon freshly ground
   black pepper

TOMATO SAUCE
2 teaspoons olive oil
1 small onion, chopped
2 garlic cloves, finely chopped
1 teaspoon dried oregano
½ teaspoon chilli flakes
sea salt and freshly ground
   black pepper
2 x 400 g cans crushed tomatoes
⅓ cup flat-leaf parsley leaves,
   finely chopped
3 tablespoons finely chopped
   basil leaves

Preheat the oven to 180°C. Line a baking tray with baking paper.

In a large bowl, use your hands to mix the turkey mince, onion, garlic, parsley, egg, oregano, salt and pepper. Form into golf ball–sized balls and place on the prepared baking tray.

Bake the meatballs for 15 minutes, or until they are firm to the touch and cooked through.

Meanwhile, make the sauce. Warm the olive oil in a large frying pan over medium heat. Add the onion and cook for about 5 minutes, or until softened and translucent. Stir in the garlic, oregano and chilli flakes, season with salt and pepper and cook for 2 minutes. Add the crushed tomatoes, bring the sauce to the boil and then simmer for 10 minutes. Stir in the parsley and basil and season to taste.

Place the meatballs in the sauce and spoon the sauce over to coat.

Tip:
Serve with a side salad of 2 cups of rocket leaves tossed with lemon juice and olive oil.

PERFECT PASTA
SALAD – *BOOM!*

PREP: **5 MINUTES** // COOK: **15 MINUTES** // **MAKE AHEAD** // SERVES: **2** // Ⓥ

225 g dried farfalle (bow-tie pasta)
150 g (1 cup) cherry tomatoes, chopped
1 small carrot, finely sliced into rounds
1 spring onion, finely sliced
2 tablespoons roughly chopped
    coriander leaves
1 avocado, diced
1 teaspoon lime juice
1 handful of mint leaves

DRESSING
1 avocado, chopped
juice of ½ lime
1 tablespoon olive oil
3 tablespoons roughly chopped
    coriander leaves
½ teaspoon ground cumin
½ teaspoon garlic powder
sea salt and freshly ground
    black pepper

Cook the farfalle in boiling salted water according to the packet directions until al dente. Drain and rinse under cold running water.

Place all of the dressing ingredients in a blender and process until smooth.

Combine the farfalle with the remaining ingredients and the dressing in a large bowl and toss gently to combine.

Tip: Refrigerate for 1 hour before serving for a refreshing cold dish.

SPICY PEANUT NOODLE SALAD

PREP: 10 MINUTES // COOK: 10 MINUTES // SERVES: 2 // Ⓥ

120 g rice noodles
1 red capsicum, deseeded and chopped
75 g (1 cup) chopped red cabbage
1 handful of mixed basil and coriander
  leaves, chopped
1 handful of chopped peanuts, to serve

SPICY PEANUT SAUCE

2 tablespoons smooth peanut butter
2 tablespoons soy sauce or tamari
  (gluten-free soy sauce)
1 tablespoon sesame oil
1 tablespoon maple syrup or honey
juice of 1 lime
1 garlic clove, peeled
1 tablespoon sriracha chilli sauce

Place all of the ingredients for the spicy peanut sauce in a food processor or blender with 2 tablespoons of water and process until smooth.

Cook the rice noodles according to the packet directions.

Toss the noodles with the veggies and herbs and enough spicy peanut sauce to coat. Sprinkle with the chopped peanuts and serve with the extra sauce on the side.

*Tip:
Enjoy this dish
hot or cold.*

POLENTA VEGGIE BOWL – *SO TASTY!*

PREP: **5 MINUTES** // COOK: **20 MINUTES** // SERVES: **2** // (V)

225 g brussels sprouts, halved
125 ml (½ cup) olive oil
2 garlic cloves, finely chopped
1 tablespoon aged balsamic vinegar
½ teaspoon sea salt, plus extra
    for seasoning
½ teaspoon freshly ground
    black pepper, plus extra
    for seasoning
190 g (1 cup) polenta
1 small red onion, finely sliced
80 g (2 cups) chopped kale leaves,
    central stems removed

Preheat the oven to 200°C. Line a baking tray with baking paper.

Toss the brussels sprouts in a bowl with 2 tablespoons of the olive oil, the garlic, balsamic vinegar and salt and pepper. Spread the sprouts over the prepared baking tray and bake, stirring occasionally, for about 20 minutes, or until crisp.

Meanwhile, cook the polenta according to the packet directions. Set aside, keeping warm.

Heat 2 tablespoons of the olive oil in a frying pan over medium–low heat. Add the onion and cook for 4–5 minutes, or until translucent, stirring occasionally. Season with salt and pepper to taste and remove from the pan. Set aside.

Using the same pan, heat the remaining olive oil. Add the kale, season with salt and pepper and sauté for 2 minutes, or until slightly wilted.

Divide the polenta between two bowls, then top with the onion, kale and brussels sprouts.

*Tip:
For creamier polenta, stir in 1 tablespoon of soft goat's cheese.*

MOREISH MUSHROOM
& LENTIL BURGERS

PREP: 8 MINUTES // COOK: 20 MINUTES // SERVES: 2 // Ⓥ

1 tablespoon ghee or coconut oil,
   plus extra for frying
1 small red onion, sliced
sea salt
2 garlic cloves, finely chopped
3 tablespoons chopped rosemary leaves
1 tablespoon thyme leaves
180 g (2 cups) sliced mushrooms
2 tablespoons soy sauce or tamari
   (gluten-free soy sauce)
75 g (½ cup) sunflower seeds
   or pumpkin seeds
500 g (2½ cups) canned green lentils,
   drained and rinsed
2 tablespoons olive oil
1 tablespoon dijon mustard
freshly ground black pepper
wholegrain rolls, to serve

TOPPINGS
cos lettuce leaves
sliced tomato
sliced cucumber
sliced red onion
sliced pickled jalapeño chillies
crumbled goat's cheese

In a frying pan over medium heat, melt the ghee or coconut oil. Add the onion and a pinch of sea salt. Cook for 5 minutes, or until softened, then add the garlic, rosemary and thyme. Cook for 1–2 minutes, then add the mushrooms. Stir occasionally for 4–6 minutes, then add the soy sauce or tamari and stir to coat. When the mushrooms are cooked, remove from the heat and set aside.

. . . .

In a food processor, blitz the sunflower or pumpkin seeds until they resemble breadcrumbs. Add the lentils, mushroom mixture, olive oil, mustard and a pinch of pepper. Pulse several times to blend. Stir and scrape down the side, pulsing again if needed. The mixture should be thick.

. . . .

Use your hands to form the mushroom mixture into six to eight patties.

. . . .

Heat some extra ghee or coconut oil in a large frying pan over medium–high heat and cook the burgers for 4–6 minutes, flipping once. Serve the burgers on wholegrain rolls with your choice of toppings.

. . . .

ENJOY!

SEARED BLUE-EYE TREVALLA
WITH HERBY PASTA

PREP: **8 MINUTES** // COOK: **20 MINUTES** // SERVES: **2**

1 x 225 g blue-eye trevalla fillet,
    or other firm white-fleshed fish
sea salt
2 tablespoons olive oil
225 g dried fettuccine
1 tablespoon butter
2 garlic cloves, finely chopped
1 teaspoon finely chopped capers
180 ml (¾ cup) double cream
280 g (2 cups) frozen peas
zest of 1 lemon
freshly ground black pepper

HERB SAUCE
1 large handful of basil leaves
1 large handful of flat-leaf
    parsley leaves
1 small handful of dill fronds
1 small handful of chives
2 spring onions, chopped into
    2.5 cm pieces
juice of ½ lemon
½ teaspoon sea salt
¼ teaspoon freshly ground
    black pepper
125 ml (½ cup) extra-virgin olive oil

To make the herb sauce, place all of the ingredients in the bowl of a food processor and process until smooth, scraping down the side of the bowl as needed. Set aside.

Next, rinse the fish, pat dry with paper towel and season with salt. Heat the olive oil in a large frying pan over medium–high heat. Sear the fish for 3–4 minutes on each side, or until it flakes easily. Transfer to a plate and use two forks to flake the fish.

Meanwhile, bring a saucepan of salted water to the boil. Add the fettuccine and cook according to the packet directions until al dente. Drain well.

While the pasta is cooking, heat a large frying pan over medium–high heat. Add the butter and garlic. Stir the garlic until lightly browned, then add the capers. Turn the heat down to low and stir in the cream and peas. Stir to warm the peas through.

Add the cooked and drained fettuccine to the pea mixture and stir thoroughly until it is coated in the cream. Add the herb sauce and stir to combine.

Divide the fettuccine mixture between two serving plates and top with the flaked fish. Sprinkle with the lemon zest and season with pepper to taste.

BUTTERY KALE SPAGHETTI
WITH SEARED SALMON

PREP: **8 MINUTES** // COOK: **15 MINUTES** // SERVES: **2**

2 x 170 g salmon fillets, skin on
sea salt and freshly ground
    black pepper
1 teaspoon ground fennel
2 tablespoons olive oil
200 g dried spaghetti
40 g (1 cup) finely chopped kale leaves,
    central stems removed
3 tablespoons finely grated parmesan
3 tablespoons pine nuts, toasted
1 tablespoon butter
lemon wedges, to serve

Season both sides of the salmon fillets with the salt, pepper and fennel. Heat a frying pan over medium–high heat, add the olive oil and lay the salmon fillets, skin-side down, in the pan. Cook for 5 minutes on the skin side, then turn over and cook for another 2 minutes. Remove from the heat and set aside.

Bring a saucepan of salted water to the boil and add the spaghetti. Cook according to the packet directions until al dente. Drain and transfer to a large bowl. Quickly add the kale while the pasta is still hot and toss, along with the parmesan, pine nuts and butter. Season with salt and lots of pepper.

Divide the spaghetti between two bowls and top each with a salmon fillet. Serve with the lemon wedges on the side.

DONE!

HERBED CHICKEN & ZUCCHINI RISONI

PREP: 5 MINUTES // COOK: 15 MINUTES // SERVES: 2

1 cup dried risoni pasta
1 large chicken breast fillet
    (about 240 g), halved horizontally
1 teaspoon dried basil
sea salt and freshly ground
    black pepper
3 tablespoons olive oil
2 zucchini, sliced into thin rounds
2 tablespoons red wine vinegar
2 teaspoons chopped dill fronds
lemon wedges, to serve

Cook the risoni in boiling salted water according to the packet directions until al dente. Drain, cover and keep warm.

Meanwhile, sprinkle the chicken with the basil and season with salt and pepper. In a large frying pan, heat 1 tablespoon of the olive oil over medium–high heat. Add the chicken and cook for 10 minutes, or until no longer pink, turning once. Remove the chicken from the pan and set aside.

In the same pan, cook the zucchini rounds over medium heat for 3–4 minutes, or until tender.

Whisk together the vinegar, remaining olive oil and the dill in a large bowl. Add the warm risoni and zucchini and toss. Season with salt and pepper.

Thickly slice the chicken and add to the risoni mixture. Gently toss. Divide the risoni mixture between two serving plates and serve with the lemon wedges on the side.

TURKEY BURGERS WITH SEASONED FRIES

PREP: **10 MINUTES** // COOK: **20 MINUTES** // **MAKE AHEAD (PATTIES)** // SERVES: **2**

225 g turkey mince (or use chicken mince if you prefer)
1 small French shallot, finely chopped
½ small jalapeño chilli, finely chopped
zest of 1 lime
2 teaspoons lime juice
2 tablespoons roughly chopped coriander leaves
1 teaspoon smoked paprika
1 teaspoon ground cumin
½ teaspoon sea salt
½ teaspoon freshly ground black pepper
olive oil, for frying

SWEET POTATO FRIES
3 small sweet potatoes, scrubbed
3 tablespoons olive oil
1 teaspoon smoked paprika
1 teaspoon ground coriander

Preheat the oven to 200°C and line two large baking trays with baking paper.

To make the fries, slice the sweet potatoes into thin, uniform fries. Toss the fries in the olive oil and spices, then spread them in a single layer over the prepared baking trays. Bake for 20 minutes, or until crisp on the outside and soft in the centre.

Meanwhile, combine the turkey mince, shallot, jalapeño, lime zest and juice, coriander, spices and salt and pepper in a bowl and use your hands to mix well. Form into four patties.

Heat a frying pan over medium heat and add a little olive oil. Fry the patties for 5 minutes on each side, or until cooked through.

Divide the fries and patties between two plates and serve.

LAMB CUTLETS
WITH PESTO
& ASPARAGUS – *YUM!*

PREP: **5 MINUTES** // COOK: **10 MINUTES** // SERVES: **2**

2 tablespoons ghee
6 lamb cutlets or loin chops
150 g asparagus (about 8 stems),
    woody ends trimmed
juice of 1 lemon
sea salt and freshly ground
    black pepper
465 g (2 ½ cups) cooked brown rice
½ cup pesto (store-bought or see
    page 234 for a recipe)

Heat 1 tablespoon of the ghee in a large frying pan over medium–high heat, add the lamb cutlets and cook for 3 minutes on each side. Remove from the heat and set aside to rest for 5–7 minutes.

Using the same pan, reduce the heat to medium–low and add the remaining ghee to sauté the asparagus for 2–3 minutes, moving the stems around to cook evenly. Remove from the heat and toss with the lemon juice and salt and pepper to taste.

Divide the rice between two plates and top with the lamb and asparagus. Dollop the pesto over the lamb and serve.

SIMPLE!

PONZU BEEF STIR-FRY
WITH ASIAN VEGGIES

PREP: **5 MINUTES** // COOK: **15 MINUTES** // SERVES: **2**

**225 g skirt steak, thinly sliced
    against the grain**
**sea salt and freshly ground
    black pepper**
½ teaspoon sesame oil
**2 spring onions, finely sliced,
    green and white parts separated**
1 garlic clove, finely chopped
2 teaspoons finely grated ginger
**1 small carrot, finely sliced
    on the diagonal**
**½ red capsicum, deseeded and
    finely sliced**
**1 small zucchini, cut into 5 mm
    matchsticks**
1 baby bok choy, quartered
**185 g (1 cup) cooked brown rice,
    to serve**
**1 large handful of coriander,
    stems and leaves, to serve**
chilli flakes, to serve (optional)

SAUCE
1 tablespoon ponzu sauce
**2 teaspoons soy sauce or tamari
    (gluten-free soy sauce)**
2 teaspoons oyster sauce
½ teaspoon cornflour

Whisk together the ingredients for the sauce and set aside.

Pat the steak dry using paper towel and season with salt and pepper. Heat a wok or large frying pan over very high heat. Add half of the steak at a time to sear, tossing occasionally, for 5–6 minutes, or until browned. Transfer to a plate and repeat with the remaining meat, then set aside.

Reduce the heat to medium–high, add the sesame oil, the white part of the spring onion, the garlic, ginger, carrot and capsicum to the pan and stir-fry for about 3 minutes, or until beginning to soften.

Add the zucchini and baby bok choy to the pan and cook for an additional 3 minutes, or until the bok choy leaves turn bright green.

Return the steak to the pan and pour in the sauce mixture. Toss to combine. Bring to the boil and allow to cook and reduce for 1–2 minutes more. Scatter with the green part of the spring onion and serve with the rice, coriander and chilli flakes (if using).

POWER
SNACKS

MEAN GREEN PROTEIN SHAKE

PREP: **6 MINUTES** // SERVES: **2** // Ⓥ

⅓ cup vanilla protein powder (some powders are thicker than others, so just add some water if it is too thick and lumpy)

3 pitted dates

2 tablespoons rice malt syrup

30 g (½ cup) chopped broccoli

45 g (1 cup) baby spinach leaves or ½ cup frozen spinach

2 teaspoons matcha green tea powder

3 tablespoons almond butter

½ avocado, chopped

2 teaspoons sea salt

500 ml (2 cups) milk of your choice, plus extra if needed

1 cup ice cubes

Place all of the ingredients in a blender and blend until super smooth. Add more liquid if it is too thick. Enjoy in two chilled glasses.

Note: This shake is a favourite of mine, packed full of vegetables and fibre. It's sweet, savoury and salty and can easily be a meal replacement. The addition of the green tea powder gives you an extra boost of energy and makes this shake even more delicious.

Pictured on page 221

Tip: My smoothies are all designed to serve two. If not consuming straight away, store in the fridge and your next snack is sorted!

COCOA-NUTTY
SMOOTHIE

Tip:
If your peanut butter is unsalted, add a little pinch of salt to the smoothie for a flavour kick.

PREP: **5 MINUTES** // SERVES: **2** // Ⓥ

2 frozen bananas, chopped
2 tablespoons cacao powder
2 tablespoons peanut butter
2 tablespoons honey or maple syrup
500 ml (2 cups) almond milk or
  milk of your choice
1 cup ice cubes

Combine all of the ingredients in a blender and blend until smooth. Divide between two glasses and serve.

Pictured on page 220

STRAWBERRY–COCONUT
SHAKE

PREP: **5 MINUTES** // SERVES: **2** // Ⓥ

300 g (2 cups) frozen strawberries
2 frozen bananas, chopped
500 ml (2 cups) coconut milk
2 tablespoons bee pollen (found in
  most health-food stores)

Combine the frozen strawberries, banana, coconut milk and 1 tablespoon of the bee pollen in a blender and blend until smooth. Divide between two glasses and sprinkle with the remaining bee pollen.

SIMPLE!

Pictured on page 220

Cocoa-nutty Smoothie
(see page 219)

Strawberry–Coconut Shake
(see page 219)

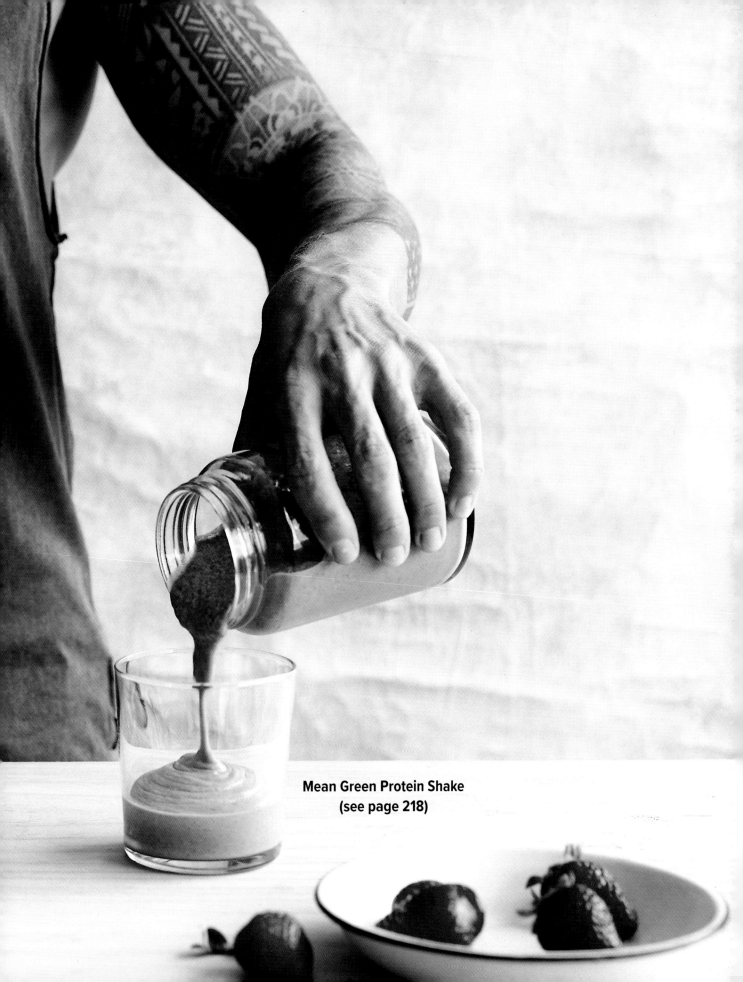

Mean Green Protein Shake
(see page 218)

PINEAPPLE POWER SMOOTHIE

PREP: **6 MINUTES** // SERVES: **2** // Ⓥ

250 ml (1 cup) coconut water
250 ml (1 cup) coconut cream
250 g (2 cups) diced frozen pineapple
pulp and juice of 4 passionfruit,
   plus extra pulp to serve
½ fennel bulb, white part only,
   roughly chopped
2 tablespoons protein powder
1 teaspoon ground turmeric
80 ml (⅓ cup) maple syrup or honey
2 teaspoons sea salt
pinch of ground star anise
fresh pineapple cubes, to serve
zest of 1 lime, to serve

Place all of the ingredients, apart from the extra passionfruit pulp, fresh pineapple cubes and lime zest, in a blender and blend for about 2 minutes until smooth and frothy. Divide between two chilled glasses and top with some extra passionfruit pulp, the fresh pineapple cubes and grated lime zest.

GREEN BANANA SMOOTHIE

PREP: **5 MINUTES** // SERVES: **2** // Ⓥ

1 banana
3 handfuls of baby spinach leaves
2 celery stalks
1 apple, peeled, cored and chopped
1 handful of ice cubes
250 ml (1 cup) water

Place all of the ingredients in a blender and blend. You may need to add more water if it's too thick. Divide between two glasses and serve.

DONE!

HONEY-BEE YOGHURT WHIP

PREP: **5 MINUTES** // SERVES: **2** // Ⓥ

375 g (1½ cups) Greek yoghurt
1 tablespoon flaxseed oil or
   light olive oil
1 teaspoon ground cinnamon
⅓ cup protein powder
1 tablespoon bee pollen (found in most
   health-food stores; substitute with
   some dried goji berries or any
   finely chopped dried fruit)
1 tablespoon flaxseeds
2 tablespoons cacao nibs
3 tablespoons honey

Place the yoghurt, oil, cinnamon and protein powder in a bowl and whisk to combine. Divide between two serving bowls, sprinkle with the bee pollen, flaxseeds and cacao nibs and finish with a generous drizzle of honey.

Tip:
Some protein powders are thicker than others, so just add a little water if it's too lumpy.

FRUIT & YOGHURT
PARFAIT

PREP: **10 MINUTES** // SERVES: **2** // **MAKE AHEAD** // (V)

375 g (1½ cups) Greek or plain yoghurt
   (or use dairy-free if you prefer)
2 tablespoons maple syrup or honey
1 teaspoon sea salt
1 tablespoon hemp seeds or
   toasted sesame seeds
3 tablespoons goji berries
3 tablespoons dried fruit of your choice
130 g (¾ cup) diced dried papaya
100 g (¾ cup) toasted muesli
2 tablespoons chopped almonds
2 tablespoons chopped cashew nuts
freeze-dried dragonfruit or passionfruit
   powder, or any freeze-dried fruit
   powder (optional; available in most
   health-food stores)
dark chocolate (80% cacao), to serve

Place the yoghurt in a bowl along with the maple syrup or honey, salt and seeds, and mix well. Layer the yoghurt mixture, berries, fruit, muesli and nuts in two short glasses.

Sprinkle with the freeze-dried fruit powder (if using) and use a peeler or grater to shave some dark chocolate over the top.

ENJOY!

Tip:
This will keep well in the fridge for several hours if you want to make it ahead of time.

NUTTY BANANA RICE CAKES

PREP: **5 MINUTES** // SERVES: **2** // Ⓥ

2 tablespoons almond butter
2 brown rice cakes
1 banana, sliced
1 teaspoon maple syrup or honey
pinch of ground cinnamon

Spread the almond butter evenly over the rice cakes, then lay slices of banana on top. Drizzle with the maple syrup or honey and sprinkle with the cinnamon.

....

SORTED!

SIMPLE YOGHURT SNACK BOWL

PREP: **5 MINUTES** // SERVES: **1** // Ⓥ

125 g (½ cup) Greek yoghurt
1 tablespoon slivered almonds
3 tablespoons fresh blueberries
1 teaspoon chia seeds
maple syrup or honey, to serve

Place the yoghurt in a bowl, top with the almonds, blueberries and chia seeds and finish with a drizzle of maple syrup or honey.

ON-THE-GO ALMOND PROTEIN BARS

PREP: **10 MINUTES** // FREEZE: **1 HOUR** // **MAKE AHEAD** // **MAKES 12** // (V)

½ cup whey protein powder
  (some protein powders are thicker
  than others; add a little water if it's
  too lumpy)
3 tablespoons sunflower seeds
65 g (½ cup) goji berries
3 tablespoons flaxseeds
2 tablespoons sesame seeds, toasted
80 g (½ cup) almonds, chopped
100 g (½ cup) dried buckwheat or
  15 g (½ cup) puffed rice
215 g (¾ cup) almond butter
3 tablespoons melted coconut oil
80 ml (⅓ cup) maple syrup or honey
2 teaspoons sea salt

Spray a 20 cm square baking tin with cooking spray and line with baking paper.

Mix all of the ingredients in a bowl and pour the mixture into the tray. Smooth out and freeze for a minimum of 1 hour.

Cut into slices and store individual pieces in zip-lock bags in the fridge for future snacks.

JOB DONE!

CHUNKY GUACAMOLE

PREP: **5 MINUTES** // SERVES: **2** //

2 avocados
1 tablespoon extra-virgin olive oil
½ teaspoon sea salt
pinch of freshly ground black pepper
½ tomato, seeds and pulp removed, finely diced
2 tablespoons roughly chopped coriander or basil leaves
juice of 1 small lemon
½ small red onion, very finely chopped

Cut the avocados in half and discard the seeds. Score the flesh with a small knife and scoop out with a spoon. Using the back of a fork, mash the avocado flesh: don't overdo it, as the guacamole should be a little chunky.

Add the remaining ingredients and stir to combine.

Tip:
Serve with corn chips, crackers or veggie sticks for dipping.

PERFECT
KALE PESTO

PREP: **10 MINUTES** // SERVES: **4–6** // (V)

80 g (2 cups) chopped kale leaves,
   central stems removed
25 g (1 cup firmly packed) basil leaves
50 g (⅓ cup) pine nuts
3 garlic cloves, finely chopped
50 g (½ cup) finely grated parmesan
125 ml (½ cup) extra-virgin olive oil
sea salt and freshly ground
   black pepper

Place the kale, basil and pine nuts in a food processor and pulse several times. Add the garlic and parmesan and pulse a few more times. Stop the machine and scrape down the side of the food processor with a rubber spatula.

Start the food processor running on medium speed and slowly drizzle in the olive oil, occasionally stopping the motor and scraping down the side. Add salt and pepper to taste and process to combine.

Transfer to a bowl and serve.

Tip:
Serve with fingers
of wholegrain
toast, veggie sticks
or crackers for
dipping.

SMOKY EGGPLANT DIP

PREP: **10 MINUTES** // COOK: **12 MINUTES** // SERVES: **4–6** // Ⓥ

2 large eggplants
2 tablespoons sunflower seeds
2 teaspoons sesame seeds
1 tablespoon pumpkin seeds
3 tablespoons olive oil, plus extra
  for seasoning
sea salt
3 tablespoons tahini
juice of ½ lemon
1 garlic clove, peeled
1 teaspoon smoked paprika
freshly ground black pepper
1 teaspoon chopped flat-leaf
  parsley leaves
toasted wholemeal or sourdough
  bread, rye crackers or any crackers
  of your choice, to serve

Heat a chargrill pan over high heat or a barbecue to hot. Poke some holes in the eggplants with a fork and place them on the grill. The idea here is to burn the outsides completely, while steaming the insides so they become soft. This takes about 10 minutes on very high heat, but you will know that it's done when the eggplants are collapsed and soft to the touch. Be careful as the steam from the insides can burn. Alternatively, you can do the same in an oven preheated to 200°C. When the eggplants are soft and completely charred, carefully remove them from the heat and transfer to a heatproof bowl to cool down. When cool enough to handle, gently peel off the burnt skin and transfer the flesh to a sieve to drain off any excess liquid.

Meanwhile, heat a small frying pan over medium heat and toast the sunflower, sesame and pumpkin seeds until golden. Add a few drops of olive oil and some salt. Mix well and set aside.

Place the eggplant flesh in a blender or food processor along with the tahini, lemon juice, a pinch of salt, the garlic and paprika. Blend well, drizzling in the olive oil until smooth. Season with salt and pepper to taste.

Transfer to a serving bowl, add the toasted seeds on top for extra fat and protein, sprinkle on the parsley and serve with some bread or crackers.

WHITE BEAN
HUMMUS – *SO GOOD!*

PREP: **10 MINUTES** // SERVES: **2** // Ⓥ

2 garlic cloves, chopped
2 x 400 g cans white beans,
    drained and rinsed
180 g (⅔ cup) tahini
3 tablespoons lime juice
3 tablespoons olive oil, plus extra
    to serve
½ teaspoon sea salt, plus extra
    (optional)
pinch of paprika, to serve

In a food processor, combine the garlic, white beans, tahini, lime juice, olive oil and salt with 125 ml (½ cup) of water. Process until smooth, then taste and add more salt if desired.

Spoon the hummus into a serving dish, drizzle with a little extra olive oil and sprinkle with the paprika.

Tip:
Serve with
some cucumber,
radish, capsicum,
celery and carrot
sticks.

MEDITERRANEAN TUNA DIP

PREP: **5 MINUTES** // SERVES: **4**

1 x 425 g can tuna in olive oil
    or water, drained
20 g (⅓ cup) chopped chives
45 g (¼ cup) chopped and pitted
    kalamata olives
2 teaspoons maple syrup or honey
1 tablespoon apple cider vinegar
2 tablespoons Greek yoghurt
1 tablespoon dijon mustard
25 g (½ cup) finely chopped baby
    spinach leaves
55 g (¼ cup) chopped marinated
    artichokes
2 tablespoons chopped spring onion
sea salt and freshly ground
    black pepper
olive oil
seed crackers or any crackers
    of your choice, to serve

Place the tuna, chives, olives, maple syrup or honey, vinegar, yoghurt, mustard, spinach, artichokes and spring onion in a bowl and mix well.

Finish by seasoning the dip with salt, pepper and olive oil to taste. Enjoy with some crackers of your choice.

Tip:
This is a great high-protein snack if you're having a big day of training!

SPICY JALAPEÑO, CHICKEN & AVOCADO DIP

PREP: **8 MINUTES** // COOK: **8 MINUTES** // SERVES: **2**

90 g (½ cup) chopped chicken breast (or use a piece of leftover cooked chicken or store-bought roast chicken)

2 tablespoons olive oil, plus extra for cooking

sea salt and freshly ground black pepper

2 avocados

zest and juice of 1 lime

3 heaped tablespoons chopped coriander leaves

2 tablespoons chopped pickled jalapeño chillies

2 salted and roasted macadamia nuts

seeded crackers or any crackers of your choice, to serve

Cook the chicken in a frying pan over high heat with a little olive oil and some salt and pepper for about 8 minutes, or until firm and juicy. Set aside to cool.

Cut the avocados in half and discard the seeds. Scoop the flesh into a bowl and use the back of a fork to mash it. Add 1 tablespoon of the olive oil, the lime zest and juice, coriander and chicken. Mix well with a spoon and add the jalapeño. Drizzle with the remaining olive oil.

Finish by finely grating the macadamias over the avocado mixture. Serve with the crackers.

QUICK CAPRESE SALAD

PREP: **5 MINUTES** // SERVES: **2** // Ⓥ

300 g (2 cups) multicoloured cherry
   tomatoes, halved
1 teaspoon sea salt
25 g (½ cup) basil leaves
2 tablespoons extra-virgin olive oil
1 tablespoon balsamic vinegar
½ teaspoon freshly ground
   black pepper
60 g fresh mozzarella, sliced

In a large bowl, combine the tomatoes and salt and set aside for
2–3 minutes.

Add the basil leaves, olive oil, balsamic vinegar, pepper and
mozzarella to the bowl and toss. Serve in a fresh bowl.

Tip:
You could also
serve this snack
as a side salad
with a Core or
Post-workout
meal.

PUNCHY EGG
& AVO SALAD

PREP: **5 MINUTES** // COOK: **9 MINUTES** // SERVES: **2** // Ⓥ

2 **eggs**
½ **avocado, diced**
1 **tablespoon finely chopped**
    red onion
1 **tablespoon finely chopped**
    red capsicum
1 **teaspoon olive oil**
1 **teaspoon red wine vinegar**
lemon juice, to taste
sea salt and freshly ground
    black pepper
1 **small handful of micro herbs,**
    to serve (optional)

Bring a small saucepan of water to the boil. Use a spoon to gently lower the eggs in and cook for 7 minutes. Cool the eggs under cold running water and peel. Chop the eggs.

Combine the chopped egg, avocado, onion and capsicum in a bowl and dress with the olive oil, red wine vinegar and lemon juice. Season with salt and pepper, toss gently and divide between two bowls. Top with a sprinkle of micro herbs, if you like.

SIMPLE!

Tip:
A full serve of
this snack makes
a great packed
lunch for work.

SMASHED ZUCCHINI
ON TOAST WITH MINT, SAUERKRAUT & FETA

PREP: **8 MINUTES** // COOK: **10 MINUTES** // SERVES: **2** // Ⓥ

2 large zucchini

2 slices of wholemeal or sourdough bread

2 tablespoons olive oil

sea salt and freshly ground black pepper

zest and juice of 1 lemon

8 mint leaves, chopped, plus extra to serve

50 g feta, crumbled

3 tablespoons chopped toasted hazelnuts

2 tablespoons sauerkraut (or use pickled cornichons if you prefer)

1 handful of snowpea shoots or alfalfa sprouts

Fill a saucepan with water and bring to the boil over high heat. Add the whole zucchini and boil for about 10 minutes, or until fork tender. Drain and set aside for 5 minutes.

....

Meanwhile, toast the bread in the oven or toaster, depending on how thick the slices are. Drizzle some of the olive oil over the toast and season with salt and pepper.

....

Place the zucchini on a chopping board and use the back of a fork or a masher to crush them. They should be very tender to the touch. Drizzle with some more olive oil, season with salt and lemon juice to taste, and add the mint. Mix well.

....

Scoop half the zucchini mixture onto each slice of toast and spread to cover. Add the crumbled feta, hazelnuts, lemon zest and some more olive oil and season with salt and pepper. Top with the sauerkraut, sprouts and some extra mint leaves.

MEGA-VEGGIE RICE PAPER ROLLS

PREP: 12 MINUTES // COOK: 1 MINUTE // MAKE AHEAD // SERVES: 2 // (V)

6 large asparagus spears,
   woody ends trimmed
1 large carrot
1 large Lebanese cucumber,
   peeled and deseeded
1 large red capsicum
1 large avocado, finely sliced
6 large rice paper sheets
95 g (¾ cup) bean sprouts
75 g (1 cup) shredded red cabbage
12 Thai or regular basil leaves
12 mint leaves
90 g (½ cup) cooked quinoa, seasoned
   with sesame oil and soy sauce or
   tamari (gluten-free soy sauce)

DIPPING SAUCE

3 tablespoons toasted sesame oil
zest and juice of ½ lime
100 ml soy sauce or tamari
   (gluten-free soy sauce)
1 tablespoon maple syrup or honey
1 tablespoon sesame seeds, toasted
2 tablespoons chopped spring onion

Blanch the asparagus for 1 minute in boiling water. Cut all of the vegetables into matchstick-sized strips.

Fill a large bowl with warm water. Make sure it is big enough to fit the rice paper sheets.

Place a single sheet of rice paper in the warm water until it starts to soften. Lay it on a wooden chopping board. Place some matchsticks of each vegetable in the centre of the bottom half of the rice paper sheet and add some avocado slices, bean sprouts and cabbage. Top with some basil and mint leaves.

Spoon a tablespoon of the seasoned quinoa over the vegetables. Fold the bottom of the paper over once to cover, then fold in the sides and keep rolling up to form a tight little package. Repeat with the remaining rice paper and ingredients to make six rolls.

Mix all of the dipping sauce ingredients together in a small bowl.

Serve the rolls with the dipping sauce on the side.

Tip:
Both the rolls
and the dipping sauce
can be kept in separate
airtight containers in
the fridge for up to
3 days, if you want to
make them ahead
of time.

SUNDAY
FUNDAY

CHOC–NUT VEGAN
ICE CREAM

PREP: 5 MINUTES // MAKE AHEAD // MAKES: 450–500 ML

4 frozen bananas, chopped
3 heaped tablespoons peanut butter
3 heaped tablespoons cacao powder
2 tablespoons maple syrup
pinch of sea salt

Place all of the ingredients in a blender and blend to a thick, creamy consistency. Eat immediately or store in an airtight container in the freezer for up to 1 month.

SIMPLE!

Tip:
If using salted peanut butter, you may not need the extra pinch of salt. Taste and be the judge!

SPICY BLACK BEAN
COOKIES – *MY TREAT!*

PREP: 5 MINUTES // COOK: 15 MINUTES // MAKE AHEAD // MAKES: 8–10

**30 g canned black beans, drained
  and rinsed**
40 g (⅓ cup) cacao powder
2 tablespoons coconut oil
**½ teaspoon cayenne pepper
  (or to taste)**
sea salt
3 tablespoons maple syrup
1 large egg
1 teaspoon natural vanilla extract
3 tablespoons chopped dark chocolate
⅓ cup cherries, pitted and chopped

Preheat the oven to 190°C. Line a baking tray with baking paper.

Place the black beans, cacao, coconut oil, cayenne and a pinch of sea salt in a food processor and blend to combine. Add the maple syrup, egg and vanilla and pulse to incorporate. The batter will be wet, but should still hold together. Remove the blade from the food processor and fold in the chopped chocolate and cherries.

Place spoonfuls of the batter on the prepared baking tray, then use a damp finger to slightly flatten. Sprinkle with a touch more salt.

Bake the cookies for 15 minutes, or until the edges start to brown. Set aside to cool, then store in an airtight container for up to 1 week.

BAKED CINNAMON APPLE
WITH LEMON YOGHURT
& TOASTY OATS

PREP: **5 MINUTES** // COOK: **25 MINUTES** // SERVES: **2**

2 large fuji apples or similar, cored and
    cut into large pieces
1 teaspoon ground cinnamon
1 tablespoon extra-virgin olive oil
juice of 1 lemon
80 ml (⅓ cup) maple syrup
1 tablespoon unsalted butter
100 g (1 cup) rolled oats
3 tablespoons toasted and
    chopped walnuts
125 g (½ cup) Greek yoghurt
zest of ½ lemon

Preheat the oven to 190°C. Line a baking tray with baking paper.

Place the apple in a bowl and add the cinnamon, olive oil, half the lemon juice and 2 tablespoons of the maple syrup and mix well. Spread the apple over the prepared baking tray. Bake for 15 minutes, until tender.

Meanwhile, melt the butter in a small saucepan over medium heat. Let it heat up without stirring it. The milk solids will start to brown, releasing a toasted caramel smell. Add the oats to the brown butter, along with the remaining maple syrup and the walnuts. Mix well with a spoon and stir constantly for 6–8 minutes, or until golden brown and slightly crispy.

When the apples are ready, remove from the oven and set aside for 5 minutes.

Divide the baked apples between two bowls and sprinkle the oat mixture over the top. Reserve the juices for the yoghurt.

In a small bowl, place the yoghurt, lemon zest, the remaining lemon juice and the juices from the baked apples and whisk to blend. Scoop a big dollop of the yoghurt mixture on top of the baked apple and enjoy!

VANILLA
& COCONUT TART

PREP: **20 MINUTES** // FREEZE: **1 HOUR** // **MAKE AHEAD** // SERVES: **4**

2 medjool dates, pitted and finely
  chopped
70 g (⅔ cup) rolled oats
2 tablespoons salted peanut butter
250 g (1 cup) Greek yoghurt
2 teaspoons maple syrup
1 teaspoon natural vanilla extract
1 tablespoon shredded coconut, toasted

Soak the chopped dates in 2 tablespoons of hot water for 10 minutes, then mash with the back of a fork.

....

Line four holes of a standard 80 ml (⅓ cup) muffin tray with baking paper or paper cases.

....

Combine the date mixture, rolled oats and peanut butter and mix well. Divide among the muffin holes and press firmly into the bases.

....

Combine the yoghurt, maple syrup and vanilla and pour evenly over the bases. Sprinkle the tops with the coconut and transfer the tray to the freezer for 1 hour, or until firm.

....

Thaw for a few minutes before serving.

....

EASY!

GOJI & ALMOND
DARK CHOCOLATE

PREP: **10 MINUTES** // COOK: **5 MINUTES** // CHILL: **30 MINUTES** // **MAKE AHEAD** // SERVES: **8**

200 g dark chocolate (at least 70% cacao)
1 tablespoon maple syrup or honey
1 tablespoon goji berries
1 tablespoon bee pollen (found in most health-food stores)
1 tablespoon hemp seeds
1 tablespoon flaked almonds

Place the chocolate and maple syrup or honey in a heatproof metal or glass bowl set over a saucepan of simmering water (don't let the bowl touch the water) and stir with a metal spoon until completely melted. Remove from the heat.

Line a baking tray with baking paper. Scatter half the goji berries, bee pollen, hemp seeds and almonds over the tray, then pour the chocolate mixture over the top and scatter with the remaining goji berries, pollen, seeds and almonds.

Place in the fridge to harden, then cut or break into eight pieces to serve. Store any leftovers in an airtight container in the fridge for up to 1 week.

THANKS

Thanks to the team at Plum: publisher Mary Small, project editor Clare Marshall and editorial assistant Ashley Carr.

Thanks to the book team: photographer Chris Middleton, stylist Lee Blaylock, chefs Caroline Griffiths and Emma Warren, designer Kirby Armstrong and editor Melody Lord.

And thanks also to:

My family – Mum, Dad, Amber and James, you guys are legends.

The big dog for giving me a shot.

David Baldwin for calling me lazy and saying he wouldn't manage me.

Sergio Perera, the Spanish bull, for teaching me how to cook and for playing a big part in developing the recipes and bringing this book to life.

Carolynn Ladd, for your great work in helping to develop the recipes, and Rocky, for all your support.

Dealburger, thanks for keeping me on track.

Cristian Prieto, for the extra shots.

INDEX

This edition published by
Brolga Publishing Pty Ltd
PO Box 12544
A'Beckett Street,
Melbourne, Victoria 8006, Australia

Email: markzocchi@brolgapublishing.com.au

A PLUM BOOK
First published in 2018 by
Pan Macmillan Australia Pty Limited
Level 25, 1 Market Street,
Sydney, NSW 2000, Australia

Level 3, 112 Wellington Parade,
East Melbourne, VIC 3002, Australia

Design by Kirby Armstrong
Edited by Melody Lord
Index by Helena Holmgren
Photography by Chris Middleton
Prop and food styling by Lee Blaylock
Food preparation by Caroline Griffiths and Emma Warren
Typeset by Kirby Jones
Colour reproduction by Splitting Image Colour Studio
Printed and bound in Malaysia by Percetakan Tatt sdn bhd

International distribution to the United Kingdom, Chris Lloyd & Associates.

We advise that the information contained in this book does not
negate personal responsibility on the part of the reader for their
own health and safety. It is recommended that individually
tailored advice is sought from your healthcare or medical
professional. The publishers and their respective employees,
agents and authors are not liable for injuries or damage
occasioned to any person as a result of reading or
following the information contained in this book.

10 9 8 7 6 5 4 3 2 1

To find out more about Luke's 12-week
interactive Zoco Body Pro program
visit zocobodypro.com

Follow Luke on social media @zocobodypro